PAUL D. EATON
15 RIVER RIDGE RD.
LITTLE ROCK, AR 72227
501-225-6603

Walking Backward in the Wind

Walking
Backward
in the Wind

HELEN MANGUM FIELDS

Texas Christian University Press
Fort Worth

Copyright © 1995 Helen Mangum Fields

Library of Congress Cataloging-in-Publication Data

Fields, Helen Mangum
    Walking backward in the wind / by Helen Mangum Fields.
        p.   cm. — (Chisholm Trail series ; no. 12)
        ISBN 0-87565-137-2 (paper)
        1. Farm life — Texas — Garza County — History — 20th century.
2. Fields, Helen Mangum — Childhood and youth. 3. Garza County
(Tex.) — Social life and customs. 4. Garza County (Tex.)— Biography.
I. Title. II. Series
F392.G3F54 1995
976.4'852–dc20

94–30503
CIP

ON THE COVER: *at left, Aunt Lizzie Mangum holding Helen Mangum Fields in her lap and, at right, Aunt Mattie Vaught. The occasion was a picnic on a hilltop at Yellow House Canyon below the Caprock northwest of Post, Texas. (Photo courtesy of the author.)*

Designed by Barbara Whitehead

Dedicated to
Lizzie Vaught Mangum
and C. J. Mangum,
my Auntie and Uncle

CONTENTS

SPRING

No West Texas child of the '20s was ever known to rush breathlessly in from out-of-doors and announce, "Spring is here! I saw a robin!" Rather, he pulled his cap more closely over his ears, buttoned his coat securely and waited for that special harbinger of spring, the bone-shattering thrust of the first sandstorm to knock him off his feet.

We could see a sandstorm coming long before it arrived. It first appeared as a dark rim just above the horizon. We kept watch over it as it inched its way upward until the western sky was inundated in a sea of sand. At this point, we knew it would not be long before the wind took command so we flew into action, making sure gates and barn doors were securely fastened and anything that might be blown around or away was safely inside.

When the storm hit, the house shook, windows rattled and any object not sturdy enough to hold its own against the onslaught went tumbling across the yard and out of sight. It was not uncommon to have neighbors return something the next day that had blown from our yard into theirs. Tumbleweeds were blown from their shallow roots, rolling across the fields and finally catching against the barbed wire fences.

At school on such days we were kept inside the sturdy walls of the red brick schoolhouse during recess periods. This made a long, tedious day and a depressing one, for there was no way to shut out the sound of the lonely, desolate wail of the wind as it swept around the corners of the building. It moaned its sad song all day long, causing us to actually look forward to the final bell and the uncomfortable walk home. It would be a miserable trip, but less so for the children living east of school — they pulled their caps down over their upturned coat collars, hugged their arms across their coat front, and let the wind carry them along. Uncle would be waiting in the car to take me home. He would drive slowly and cautiously for it was impossible to see more than a few feet on the road ahead.

Inside was the only place to be during a sandstorm. Animals knew when one was coming and hurried to their shelters. The cows huddled in the barn and the mules stood head-first in their shed, their back parts bearing the brunt of the wind and sand. A few brave hens might dare to stay outside their house and end up looking like peacocks with feathers inverted above their bodies.

Sometimes a feather would blow off and disappear into the wind.

It would blow relentlessly all day. Uncle, sitting disconsolately by the window, watched as the wind scooped soil from his farm, and deposits of sand, which had been some other farmer's soil, collected in the furrows.

All plans for the day were put aside. It was too uncomfortable to go outside. Grains of sand bore into your exposed skin, into your eyes so it was next to impossible to see where you were going, up your nose so every breath filled your throat and lungs. If Uncle had to go outside to take care of some unavoidable chore he tied a handkerchief around his nose and mouth, pulled a stocking cap over his head and buttoned his mackinaw securely.

Late in the afternoon the wind slowly subsided and finally came to a standstill. The anemic sun was a pale outline through the settling dust; then, as the sky quickly cleared, it shone brightly, as if nothing unusual had been going on.

Now the cleaning up began. No house was built that would keep out the fine powdery dust; it sifted in through every crack and crevice. Houses back then had no weather stripping nor any of the sealing material we have today. Cleaning up after a sandstorm was a monumental task. The window ledges were piled neatly with sand, bed spreads were covered, it had collected on baseboards. The dishcloths Auntie had used in the kitchen to cover anything setting out on the cabinet or table had to be removed carefully. Every piece of furniture must be dusted and every floor swept. Often a gallon or more of sand would be carried out after the dusting and sweeping. Auntie would sometime say, "I've a mind to just leave this for it will likely come another one tomorrow." But we never did; we always had the house spick-and-span by nightfall.

The wind always blows in West Texas — at least, it did when I was growing up on a Garza County farm in the '20s. The wind, and how it blew, determined our daily activities: how the farm crops grew and were harvested, how we dressed and how we lived in general. The blowing wind was considered a normal weather condition, an ever-present force. When it did not blow we were all a little uneasy.

Most of the time it would blow just to be blowing and with a fierceness that took away one's breath. To walk backing into the wind was something all West Texas kids learned to do. It was not difficult since there was nothing to stumble or fall over — no trees, no hills, no streams of water — only a flat, level plain with an unbroken horizon stretching to infinity, where wind swept at will across fields and farmyards, moaning as it whipped around houses and barns, the school building, churches and Mr. Parrish's store. It snatched thoughtlessly at scarves, caps, schoolbooks, set farmers' hats sailing out of reach, and had women holding frantically to skirts to keep them in their proper place.

Winters would not have been so bitterly cold but for the incessant wind that whipped every cold draft into a blue norther and every snowfall into a blizzard. Summers were plagued with hot burning winds that scorched the cotton crops, dried up the gardens and seared one's skin; fall of the year was more calm than any season. But come March and the first days of spring, the wind would show off like a spoiled, unruly child.

March has stayed true to its reputation, not improving much through the years. The poet described March perfectly when she wrote "Summer's his mother; winter's his father. Having had him, they wanted no other." Then, as now, one day warm and balmy and the next day frigid and windy. The weather could change within the hour from one extreme to the other out in West Texas. It put us in a quandary how to plan a day or how to dress.

On one of those surprisingly warm mornings when the sun rose in a clear blue sky, the wind lying back like a sleeping baby, I would beg Auntie to let me leave off my long underwear. The answer was a firm, close-the-subject "No." Then could I leave off my heavy coat and wear just a sweater? Sometimes I won the battle, but it was an empty victory. I'd go happily off to school feeling pounds lighter with my sweater keeping me snug and warm, but by morning recess I was already regretting my decision, for the wind was picking up. By noon it was blowing full force, cutting clear to my bones through the flimsy protection of my sweater.

We children would gather on the south side of the school building where we caught the sun and were protected from the north wind. We'd eat our lunch quickly and then huddle together, hoping for an early bell calling us back to the classroom. The boys were braver and hardier and their trousers kept them warmer, so they were more likely to continue with games and fun than we girls.

By the time school was out we would be facing a cruelly cold trip home. Uncle would be waiting in the Model-T Ford to drive me the two and half miles home, the isinglass curtains on the sides of the car ballooning in and out with the wind.

The next day there was no argument; I wrapped up in my winter coat only to have it turn off so warm we school kids were shedding every garment we decently could.

5

Though the thermometer could not be relied upon, one thing we were certain of — the wind would blow. Anytime through the year the wind blew erratically one of the aunts would say, "It's just like March today."

We were typical West Texas dry-land farm folk — totally dependent upon what the farm-produced. Our income came from the cotton crop, the butter and egg money, the sale of pigs, chickens and other farm-produced commodities. Yet, I doubt any of us ever felt poor or disadvantaged. We had everything we needed.

Ours was a simple farm, very much like all the other farms in Garza County during the 1920s. The house, square as a child's building block, was comfortably crouched like a plump mother hen contentedly hovering over her brood. Painted cream and trimmed with green, it presented a neat, friendly appearance. Beyond the backyard lay a long, low red barn to accommodate the mules, horses and cows and to store the grain and the harness and other items necessary to the well-being of the animals. The hog pen, for aesthetic reasons, was located as far away from the farmyard and house as possible, at the northeast corner beyond the orchard. But when the wind blew from the east the orchard was no protection from the bad smell. Other out-buildings were a chicken house, a corn crib, brooder houses, a privy, garage, windmill and overhead storage tank for water. This, more or less, was the outlay for all the farms in the area.

Turning onto the graded county dirt road that ran east and west in front of our house, we could see it gradually diminish into the eastern horizon on its way toward town. At the top of the Caprock, where the land suddenly dropped a few hundred feet to the lowlands, we could see Post snugly nestled against the skyline, the tall stack of the

Postex cotton mill pointing to the sky. The road dropped steeply down with rough hills and gullies on either side of it until we reached the level ground below. Here the land was covered with buffalo grass, mesquite trees and scrub cedars. Quite a contrast to our neat, cultivated fields on the plains above.

People from all the surrounding communities gathered at Post to transact business and legal matters. Down the center of town ran Main Street; a broad street, paved with brick and divided by an esplanade. On either side were businesses — Mason's Furniture Store, Greenfield Hardware, two drugstores, a bakery, a cafe, First National Bank, the Garza Theater, Doughty's Racket Store, Stevens Dry Goods, Bryant Link and several others. Main Street also acted as a division point in the town's social structure.

Mr. Childress' grocery store sat on one of the side streets across the street from Mr. Cox's lumber store. We did all our grocery trading with Mr. Childress. He bought Auntie's butter and eggs and she bought what groceries she needed from him. He sat on a stool behind the counter, the baking powder, salt, sugar, flour, soda, flavorings, raisins and such items stacked neatly on shelves behind him. Across the room were other things such as oranges, lemons, apples, a stalk of bananas hanging from the ceiling, and on more shelves against the far wall, rice, oatmeal, Post Toasties, tea, coffee and other items necessary to shoppers. Auntie took her neatly written list from her purse and read it item by item to Mr. Childress: Baking powder. Mr. Childress reached behind him and got a can of Calumet from the shelf. Dozen oranges. Mrs. Childress, in her floor-length checked dress with a large Mother Hubbard apron covering it, took a brown paper sack from the counter, reached into the crate of oranges sitting in the middle of the store and counted out twelve, dropping them into the bag and placing it beside the baking powder. Box of raisins. Mr. Childress walked down the row of shelves and took down a box, placing it on the counter. Finally, Auntie's list was exhausted and her purchases rung up on the cash register. Then as she looked on, Mr. Childress deducted the amount from the total he owed her for butter and eggs, and gave her the difference in cash. After this was satisfactorily settled, the groceries were stacked in the wooden box she had brought the produce in, then placed under the counter for us to pick up on our way home.

While Auntie and I were attending to our shopping Uncle had taken our can of cream by the produce house to sell. He had shopping of his own to do — a block of salt for the cows or a piece he needed to repair a fence or plow or he might have business at the bank or courthouse. Also, time was spent out on the sidewalk in front of the businesses, visiting with neighbors and friends who were in town for the same reasons we were. Going to town was an important part of our social life.

There were times when Auntie needed hemstitching done on a piece she was making — a table runner, a scarf, a dress she was making for me or a special pair of pillowcases. In this case, as soon as we were finished at Mr. Childress' store we walked straight up the sidewalk to the little hotel on the corner of Main Street. This is where Clara Brown had a handwork shop and a machine on which she did beautiful hemstitching. She had a little girl, Lorrena, my age. Besides being a nice playmate, Lorrena had a tricycle and generously allowed me to ride it as much as I wanted to. The shop was upstairs in one of the hotel rooms and the long wide corridor which ran the length of it was a perfect place to ride. Mrs. Brown did the hemstitching while the customer waited, so if there were other ladies ahead of Auntie that meant more rides on the tricycle. It was a highlight of my Saturday, a special treat I could brag about to my schoolmates on Monday. Not many of us had such an opportunity for, as a rule, country kids did not own tricycles.

At the east end of Main Street stood the Algerita Hotel, the last building before the railroad tracks. It was a long, narrow two-storied wooden building with many windows and gables. On the side that fronted toward the railroad and depot were two balconies. Painted brown with white trim, the hotel was unlike any other building in our experience. To us country kids, none of whom had ever so much as set foot inside its lobby, it was a glamorous gathering place of adventure, far-away places and mysterious intrigue — exciting to walk past and to speculate upon but totally divorced from our own experience.

Almost always when we were in town a Santa Fe passenger train came through. This was pure excitement of the highest type! Before we could see it we could hear it chug-chugging on the rails and hear its long warning whistle as it reached the last crossing before coming into full view. It pulled into the station, bell ringing, smoke billowing from its stack, and brakes complaining noisily as it came to a stop beside the depot. Station hands quickly fell into action, pulling their wagons on the run past the passenger cars to the baggage car where they would unload boxes, bundles and trunks. These high wooden-wheeled wagons, a quarter the size of a regular wagon, were called station wagons and were pulled by hand. One was pulled up close to the mail car, where postal employees would accept the first-class mail, packages and parcels and deposit the local mail with the Santa Fe postal superintendent. The car attendants set out the steps and up and down the train passengers would be getting off; when anxious eyes spotted them, relatives and friends rushed up with open arms to greet them. A traveling salesman or a lone passenger would descend from one of the cars and look speculatively and curiously around him, taking the measure of our little town. The conductor, first off the train, walked up and down the station platform, consulting his huge pocket watch from time to time. Eventually, at the correct moment, he called out, "All aboard!" Departing passengers picked up their luggage and started moving toward the train. There was a flurry of last-minute hugs and kisses before they climbed the steps and were lost from sight, only to appear at one of the windows to wave a final goodbye. Train porters removed the steps, the conductor swung on board and waved his signal to the engineer. The huge engine belched loudly as it took a big gulp of steam and began slowly moving off down the track, gathering speed as it rounded the curve and headed east, giving one last whistle as it made a crossing and disappeared from sight. This was another Saturday treat which could be savored and remembered all week long.

The Postex Mill was the life blood of Post. C. W. Post built it when he founded Post and developed farming and ranching in Garza County. The mill took the cotton which was grown on the farms above the Caprock and the "sandy land" farms below the Cap and processed it through all the stages necessary to produce top-quality sheets and pillowcases. About two hundred fifty people were employed at the mill. The mill whistle blew early in the morning when the night shift went off and the first shift of the day reported, again at high noon and to announce any shift changes throughout the twenty-four hours a day the mill operated. At rare times, when the wind was from the east, we could hear the whistle at our farm eight miles west of town.

Across the railroad tracks and beyond the mill were the houses occupied by the few black families that lived in Post. Most of the mill hands lived in "south-town" — south of Main Street. Several blocks west of the business district the broad brick-paved Main Street became the elite residential area known as Silk Stocking Row because most of Post's fine houses stood on either side of its esplanade. Churches were sprinkled around the residential part of town and standing on one of its quiet streets was a hospital, named for Dr. Ponton, its founder. On our way out of town we passed down the street where the elementary and high school buildings stood. And somewhere there was located the post office, fire station, courthouse and the water wagon. The water wagon, pulled by a sturdy team of horses, sprayed water over the hot, dusty streets in the summer time. A gaggle of shouting, laughing kids ran after it, cooling their bare feet and making a lark of it.

Post was a wide-awake little town, boasting probably two thousand people during those early prosperous days. Cotton was king and cattle ranchers owned and operated big spreads, driving their cattle to Fort Worth or Kansas City to market, bringing back more wealth to spread around. They were good days, orderly and predictable, an environment we expected would go on forever — for our lifetime, at least.

We left town on Saturday when we were finished with

business and shopping and "street" visiting. We drove west out of town and were soon in the country. Looking back, I watched a curl of dust rise behind us as our Model-T Ford chugged over the narrow rutted road, picking up speed as we approached the steep incline that reached up the side of the Caprock. This was the dreaded part of the trip for me. My apprehension grew with every turn of the wheels. It was my fearful conviction the car would stall and roll back into the ditch on the north side of the road where the deep cut was made when the road was built. I was convinced, should this happen, we would never be seen or heard of again. There were times when the Model-T refused to climb. Then Uncle would let it roll back down and take a fresh start. It was necessary at times to turn the car around and back up the hill. One of the peculiarities of a Model-T was that it could pull a hill easier traveling in reverse — we proved the fact more than once.

As we reached the top and leveled out we got our first glimpse of the unending vista spreading out in all directions. Miles and miles of flat plains lay green in the midst of summer, brown in the midst of fall and stark in the midst of winter.

The land was geometrically laid out in one-mile blocks with farm homes dotting the landscape all along the county roads. After we made the jog at the corner where the dozen or more windmills stood to pump water for the town folk, we drove west as straight as an arrow for five miles, passing farms along the way — Meador's farm at the second crossroad, on by Henderson's and Bullard's. Then we could see it, the late afternoon sun wrapping its golden rays around our own special place — home.

First, the small plot where the alfalfa grew, then the orchard, the garden, the front yard and then turn in to the big gate. "Jump out and open the gate," Uncle said. And Auntie added, "Run see if there is any mail in the box." By this time Old Chill had discovered we were home, yelping and jumping on me, running circles in front of the car. We would drive through the gate, between the rows of locust trees, and come to a stop in front of the garage so we could unload the car. The familiar sounds and smells and sights engulfed us in a circle of warmth.

The fragrance of roses and honeysuckle from the front yard mingled pleasantly with the odor of manure from the barnyard. The mules nickered and moved toward the fence asking for their bundles of hay. We could hear the clang of Bonnie's bell as she came up the lane from the pasture, the other cows following her in single file. Fat white hens ambled about the yard pecking at whatever hens find on the ground to peck at. Roosters strutted about overseeing the hens. The cats came scampering and meowing, getting tangled in our feet as we went through the back door.

It was a good kind of homecoming — knowing the animals were glad to see us, feeling the warmth of their faithful affection. Farm animals are friends; they encircle their human family with undemanding, serene acceptance. They have a quiet dignity, never groveling for attention but displaying a certainty in their relationship that brings out the best in a person.

Getting home was always the best part of any day when we had been to town or visiting friends or relatives. It seemed especially so when we had spent the day in Post, the county seat. Farm kids needed the openness of the country after the confinement, noise and strange smells of town.

In April the wind gave up its push and pull and soft-ened to a gentle caress, and we school girls began thinking about taking off our long black stockings and winter underwear. We thought about it — our parents thought differently. There was still a chill in the air; there could be one more norther up Nature's sleeve. So came the wait-ing, daily asking, until finally around the middle of April the first knee socks made their appearance on the school ground. One of my best memories is the indescribable, delicious feeling of the light, sweet wind gently stroking my bare knees on the first day I was allowed to wear my socks. It gave me a giddy feeling of freedom unlike any other sensation.

All winter long we had been encumbered by and enshrouded in layers of clothing, systematic and exacting in their arrangement. Our long underwear was not the shear, warm, convenient two-piece garment we know today. The sleeves and legs had no neatly woven ribbing around wrist and ankle. It was a one-piece garment made from heavy ribbed-knit cotton fabric, buttoned down the front and a fly at the back held up with three large buttons. It denied the body any pretense to grace or beauty.

The long underwear, a unisex garment, suitable for either a boy or girl, was worn next to the body. Over this garment, for us girls, came black sateen bloomers followed by the underskirt. Auntie made mine from white muslin, the scooped out neck and armholes trimmed with lace. Over the underskirt went the dress or skirt and sweater. However, this was not the end; next came the long black ribbed cotton stockings. It was a tedious technique to pull the stockings over the leg of the underwear. The test was to fold the leg neatly and hold firmly in position until the stocking could be pulled up. I never accomplished this on the first try, seldom on the second and usually, in exasperation, stuffed my leg into the stocking any way I could. The results was a lumpy, deformed-looking appendage. Shoes laced above the ankles. Coat, scarf, gloves and cap completed the ensemble. Boys fared better for their overalls covered their underwear legs. Their caps had ear flaps, and they wore heavy wool mackinaws.

Happy the day when Auntie and other mothers gave the word and these awkward clothes were put off. Our bodies felt light as feathers. However, it was not until after Easter had come and gone that the toboggan cap was replaced with a silk scarf and the cotton dresses came out of the closet.

Easter, I learned many years later, is the first Sunday after the first full moon following the spring equinox. I don't know why I failed to learn this until so late in life for, back then, farm folk laid the almanac next to the Bible on the front room table, and, in many cases, read it more frequently and avidly. They referred to it for answers concerning weather, dates, proper planting schedules and methods, full moon and other important information. Being forewarned of the exact date of Easter, our preparations began well in advance of Easter Sunday.

One of the forerunners of this special celebration was the arrival in our rural mail box of the new spring and summer Sears & Roebuck and Montgomery Ward catalogs. This was our signal to get on with Easter preparations. Prominent in our hopes and dreams were a new hat, new dress (mine was often made of pongee) and new patent leather shoes. The boys, I expect, were just as hopeful of a new suit or pants or jacket and shoes. All these things could be purchased from the catalogs. Since I was never with my boy cousins at this time of year, I do not know if they studied the Sears & Roebuck and Montgomery Ward as avidly as did the girls.

On the day the catalogs arrived, as soon as supper dishes were put away, Auntie and I settled down together at the library table in the front room under the glow of the Aladdin lamp, to a long satisfactory session with first one then the other of the new catalogs.

Every turn of the page brought exclamations of delight. When we came to the hat section my eyes searched eagerly for a pink one. I longed for a pink hat — preferably decorated with lots of ribbons and flowers — all pink. But Auntie in her kindly persuasive way could always convince me that pink was not my best color. She was right. My hair, straight as a stick and black as a crow, cut in a Buster Brown style, and big brown eyes, set in a little dark-complexioned face, would be ridiculously lost under all the frills and furbelows of such a pink confection. I settled, if not enthusiastically, in good humor, for a black straw sailor hat with long grosgrain streamers hanging down the back. Auntie may have been a farm woman but knew how to dress me in good style.

My shoes would be black patent leather slippers with a strap across the ankle that buttoned on the side. Another of my unfulfilled longings was to own a pair of Roman sandals. Some of my friends and my cousin Joan had them, and to my mind they were in every way superior to slippers. They were made to extend above the ankle and had a series of thin straps that started at the instep and progressed up every inch or so to the top, each strap fastened on the side with a button. Auntie thought they were tacky. She convinced me that slippers were THE thing because, she pointed out, Miss Wilma wore PUMPS, clearly implying they were one and the same.

Miss Wilma Pirtle, who must have been all of twenty years old, was my idol. She was a pretty blue-eyed blonde, wore beautiful clothes and always made a fuss over me. I named my favorite paper dolls Wilma and in my fantasy pretended to be her. Auntie put the clincher on her argument by saying, "You'll look just like Miss Wilma." After that nothing in the world would have induced me to have anything but slippers — until I arrived in church Easter morning and saw two of my friends walking down the aisle in shiny new Roman sandals. My slippers dwindled into the commonplace compared to such glamour.

Every wardrobe held a spring coat; this was a necessity, not a luxury. The weather was too cool to go without one; the winter one was too heavy. A spring coat was a special purchase we could not expect every year for, like the winter coat, hems and sleeves were let down for as many seasons' wear as possible.

One year my coat was a complete departure from the normal. Auntie and I, with one of her friends, went on a shopping trip to Slaton, a town twenty miles or more northwest of our farm. It was a larger town than Post and had a nice department store which was a real shopping mecca compared to Bryant Link and Stevens Dry Goods in Post. All menswear and dry goods were downstairs. A mezzanine, where the ladies and girls ready-to-wear was located, lay in a complete circle above the lower floor. There was a polished wood railing around the open stairway so that it was safe to walk around it and look down on the heads of sales clerks and customers — an uncommon sight and very entertaining which goaded one into an overwhelming urge to spit.

In the girls section there were dresses, hats, purses and everything the heart could desire or imagine. It was here that Auntie saw and bought for me a most charming red wool knit cape. It had a white angora collar and an attached hood rimmed with a circle of angora that perfectly framed my face. This unusual garment created quite a sensation among my peers when I walked into church that Easter Sunday morning.

We were not always so charmingly dressed on Easter Sunday. On years when the farms did not produce a crop to harvest because of some misfortune of weather or circumstances, it was a different story. We polished our school shoes and took last year's hat off the closet shelf. No pongee dress that year, unless we could still fit into last year's. More than likely, we'd wear the same Sunday dress we had been wearing all winter. If our spring coat had already been let out to the ultimate yet the sleeves were inches above our wrist and the hems faced but still too short, we had to bear up to wearing our winter coat. At least we'd be warm and comfortable instead of covered with goose bumps as we usually were in our lightweight coats.

On these years we paid strict attention to the worship service, piously consoling ourselves that it was a High Holy Day and our duty to pay attention to the minister and participate in singing "He Arose," cringing as the soprano section screeched out the high notes. Later, we would sit transfixed as we listened to Miss Wilma sing her solo, forgetting about our old hat and polished school shoes as we lost all consciousness to anything but the pure, clear notes filling our little church.

We did not complain about, nor mind too much, these lean years for we were all in it together. It was always that way. When crops were good we all prospered; when they failed we all endured. Of course, some were better farmers than others, just as one storekeeper may be a better merchant than one down the street, and some farmed larger farms than others. Regardless, when crops failed we were all equal.

At school we were busy with colored construction paper cutting out Easter baskets, rabbits and eggs and coloring designs on them with our Crayolas. When we'd made sufficient number we strung them around the walls and across windows. With justifiable pride we looked about the room at our gayly colored handwork blocking out the drab walls — very satisfied with our accomplishment. The cheerful, inviting atmosphere blotted out the long weeks of winter and brought spring right into our classroom.

On Good Friday the lower grades were treated to an egg hunt. It was held in the open pasture across the road and east of the school ground, Winder's cotton gin less than a quarter mile away at the far end.

Each child was required to bring a dozen colored eggs to school for the hunt. It was too much to expect that every pupil in grades one through six would arrive at school that morning with a dozen hard-boiled, colored eggs intact. Some would meet with accidents — intentional and unintentional. Inevitably, some would be squashed as two scruffy boys settled a fuss, hunger pangs would win out in some cases, some would be cracked when a mischievous boy grabbed a girl's basket and in the ensuing scuffle a half dozen fell out on the ground and broke. All the angry words and tears would not put them together again. Just the excitement of the occasion was enough to cause clumsiness and accidents. Such an unaccustomed break with routine kindled an exuberance that was likely to break out any time, any place. In spite of all the hazards, however, there were plenty of eggs to hide.

Several mothers from each class came early in the afternoon to hide the eggs. When time came for the hunt, the teachers walked their pupils across the road to the pasture. After all were assembled the signal was given to start the hunt. Most of us ran wildly about looking frantically this way and that hoping to see the bright-colored eggs among the mesquite trees, cacti, tall clumps of dead weeds, sedge brush and dry buffalo grass.

There were two prizes to be won; for finding the most eggs and for finding the specially marked egg. Year after year Juanita Jones won the prize for finding the most eggs. Once I whined to Auntie, pouting because I'd never won the prize. "Why does old Juanita always find the most? She must cheat!" I remarked petulantly.

"No, she doesn't cheat. She is just smarter than the rest of you."

"Why do you say that?" I asked, more than a little indignant over this comparison.

"Because while the rest of you are rushing and pushing each other and racing around like a chicken with its head off, she walks slowly behind and picks up all the eggs you leave."

Obviously, Juanita deserved to win the prize. But the same thing would happen at next year's hunt; it seemed so poor-spirited to lag along behind when everyone else was out ahead.

On Saturday, following Good Friday and the egg hunt, a norther or a sandstorm or a totally unexpected rain would set in. By Sunday, riding on a brisk wind, the temperature had dropped remarkably, making a mockery of

pushing to get near him for his pats and hugs. He trained them to pull a plow and a wagon and to obey his commands. They were a splendid team.

In 1937, after Uncle finally succumbed to selling them and buying a tractor, he was in town one day when he saw a truckload of mules parked on the street. He walked over to see them, out of curiosity and, no doubt, nostalgia. One of the mules nickered, then nickered again as Uncle's eyes searched him out. To his amazement it was Jack; gray around the ears and on his great nose, but definitely Jack. He had recognized Uncle. I was away at college by that time, but Auntie wrote me about it and how touched Uncle was with the unexpected meeting. It makes one wonder what went on in the mind of an old mule who recognized his beloved master and what memories it undoubtedly aroused in Uncle.

C. W. Post, of cereal fame, opened up the prairie land of Garza County. Before the settlers came, he laid out the farms, divided the one-mile-square blocks of land down the middle so that the crop rows were one-half-mile long. It took a steady hand and a clear mind to plow a straight row for half a mile, but Uncle did it over and over. Any farmer knows if he looks back over his shoulder, or is distracted in any way, he pulls the lines on the harness the direction in which he looks, and in so doing causes the team to turn slightly and so plow a crook into the row. When Uncle plowed he looked straight ahead between Jack and Dinah's heads. He could not abide a crooked row in his field. Passing by other farms and seeing crooks and bows, he would shake his head in chagrin and say, "Crooked as a dog's hind leg." One could look down Jake Mangum's rows and never see a bow or a bobble; straight as an arrow.

Nevertheless, straight rows or crooked, the plains of West Texas, when we had favorable weather conditions and the crops grew and flourished, were beautiful beyond description. Green as far as the eye could see — one vast, verdant landscape rolling on and on, finally disappearing over the rim of the horizon.

By the end of April planting was under way. If we had sufficient rain and snow through the winter it was undertaken with confidence knowing there was enough moisture in the soil to bring up the crop. If it had been a dry winter, then it was done with an eye to the weather, hopeful of early spring rain.

We were always preoccupied with the weather but it was after the crops were planted that the concern became an obsession. Weather was the most important element in farm life. It determined how life went on.

There must be winter rain and snow in order to have moisture to plant the crops in spring. There must be enough spring rain to "bring up" the crops. There must be enough rain throughout the summer growing season to keep the crops from dying. When the crop, by some miracle, safely reached maturity, we prayed it would not hail or come a hard beating rain that would destroy it. Few farm experiences are more tragic than having to stand helplessly by while hail beats down healthy green plants, mutilating them.

Other than the unpredictability of rain, there were other possible disasters. A sandstorm, for one thing, coming at a critical time, could inflict total destruction. When all conditions were favorable and the seed germinated on schedule and a good stand of cotton and feed stuff lay like green ribbons down the center of the long brown furrows, a sandstorm could bury the tender young plants under an accumulation of powder-fine sand, or whip them about until they were broken and bruised.

If we were spared from sandstorms and there was sufficient rain in June to keep the crops growing, we still must get by the hot winds of July. The plants would grow and flourish until they looked like rows of healthy teenagers ready to burst into full maturity. At this vulnerable stage the devastating hot winds from the south would begin their relentless blowing. Several days of this searing heat and the leaves on the cotton plants, corn, maize and other crops began to droop. Unless rain came or a shift in the wind, things went from bad to worse and finally, the crops withered and dried.

The threat of boll weevils was always hanging over us since we were years away from crop dusting and pesticides. Once grasshoppers, in a great sweep across the plains, destroyed every green thing in their path. They stripped the tall cotton stalks of their leaves and the squares from which the bolls developed and badly damaged the feed crops.

The weather was our adversary and our ally; the architect of our feast-or-famine existence. It determined whether we had seed for next year's planting; whether the payment was made on the mortgage; whether we bought new curtains for the front room, a spring hat, a new plow or a load of coal to keep the heating stove going through the last cold spell. The weather determined whether we made a crop and the crop determined our income.

It even dictated our social life. Sandstorms slowed down our activities, snow brought them to a standstill and when it rained we stayed home, inside, and watched — standing transfixed at the window savoring the experience. None of us had rainwear except Uncle. He had a slicker in case he had to get out in the rain to take care of an emergency. An umbrella salesman would have starved to death in West Texas. The only umbrella I can remember from my childhood was a black one Mrs. Ellis held over her head in summer to keep off the sun and this was only on days when the wind was at bay. West Texas wind could make short work of an umbrella. Someone gave me a shiny Chinese umbrella that was used as a toy and older cousins used it as a back drop when making snapshots of each other.

To add problem to problem, the roads were impassable when it rained and when the snow melted. Unpaved, the road surface became a sticky, soggy quagmire so that a car slipped and slid out of control and dug deep ruts to get stuck in. Horse-drawn vehicles bogged down, too.

A farmer's life was fraught with insecurities, yet there were more satisfactions than frustrations. Most years were productive. It was a good life, a challenge to any other lifestyle. A farmer was a free man — his own superior. He decided how and when he would plow and plant, reap and sell; his decisions were the final word. He lived with the continual manifestations of God — sprouting plants, a newborn calf, the sweep of the wind, the roll of thunder during a summer storm, the soft nicker of a mule, a field of stars on a crisp December night, the warm clasp of a neighbor's hand. On a West Texas farm in the twenties a man was king of his own little province.

In the busy month of May Mr. Brandon's blacksmith shop, located at the north boundary of the school ground, was a beehive of activity. Keeping a sharp edge on a plowshare was of utmost importance, so with spring planting in full swing there was a constant flow of farmers coming and going at the blacksmith shop. They brought in dull plowshares and took them away shiny and sharp, never realizing what a hardship this activity brought to a schoolhouse full of students stricken with spring fever. On a balmy spring day the most difficult task a country kid had to do was sit at his desk after noon recess and listen to the melodious, rhythmic ring of an anvil float through the open windows of the classroom. The ring of the hammer on the anvil struck a chord in our being that created an awareness we had no words for; a kaleidoscope of visions — past, present and unknown; a bittersweet seduction of our senses. No music ever written can equal the sweet note of an anvil; all long-ago farm children will tell you so. Like an opiate it rendered us drowsy, dreamy, reluctant to move, and as the notes faded away, fretfully impatient to be done with the confinement of school.

The last month of school was spent in a flurry of activity. Of first concern were our "lessons." The reader must be finished before the last day of school. As well, all the problems in the arithmetic book must be solved, the drawing book completed, the spelling list spelled. Learning was our first concern, but hanging tantalizingly over our enforced academics was the anticipation of the end-of-school program — the special ingredient that made those last days tolerable. Like a bright gauzy cloud it wove in and out among our recitations, thoughts and activities.

The program — spelled with a capital P — was one of the highlights of the year. Every child enrolled in school had some part to perform, and proud parents were eager to see them do their pieces. There was nothing haphazard about the preparation of this event; it was planned and coordinated with great care. It took place on two successive weeks — for the lower grades on a Friday night around the first week in May; on the following Friday night the upper grades put on their three-act play.

The lower grades, one through six, were organized into one big extravaganza. Of course, all told, there were no more than sixty or seventy of us. A theme was selected and worked out through skits, music, singing, recitations and dances. Our dancing was no more than merely walking through patterns the teachers painstakingly choreographed. The program also involved the mothers, for costumes had to be made. Crepe paper was a staple for both costumes and stage props.

In my first performance I was a fairy, as were the rest of the girls in my class. Our costumes, made from white crepe paper, had gathered skirts and sleeveless waists. Around the armholes, neck and waist were bands of sparkling, silvery spangles. We carried wands with silver stars on the ends. The stars were cardboard covered with tinfoil saved from gum wrappers and Hershey candy bars. We did our "dance" in a line across the stage, ending with a deep bow, our wands extended toward the audience. It was my first taste of the big time, a heady experience from which I never recovered. Thereafter, recitations for family gatherings and adult visitors seemed trite and childish.

One year we had a maypole dance with an equal number of boys and girls participating. It is hard to imagine how the teachers talked farm boys into holding pink streamers and cavorting around the pole, weaving in and out. The only explanation being that in the '20s when the teacher spoke we listened and did what she said OR ELSE. In those days children obeyed their parents and teachers, and the two worked together for the highest good of the children. Adult authority was a very desirable, wholly satisfactory practice for growing, learning children. It took the stress of responsibility off our shoulders and gave us a sense of security; the feeling of being cared for. Decisions were made for us that we had no business making for ourselves, giving us a carefree freedom that is the rightful heritage of children.

At first, we girls were thrown into fits of laughter when the boys skipped around the pole, clutching the delicate streamers in rough, work-toughened hands, but Miss Riley and Miss Hennington quickly brought order by quelling our mirth with some well-placed rhetoric. From then on we stifled our giggles behind our hand or stuffed our handkerchief into our mouth. To see those rough-and-ready boys, who usually were playing baseball, shooting marbles, fighting or chasing one of us with a worm or snake, in such an unfamiliar role was something to marvel at. But on the night of the performance, the boys, dressed in their Sunday pants, the legs folded into white knee socks (to simulate knee pants) and white ruffled shirts, which must have taken their mothers hours to make, they presented the illusion of another age, another world. The girls wore long, full-skirted dresses in rainbow colors. If brogan shoes and school oxfords looked out of place with all the finery, no one noticed or commented.

The maypole was set up east of the school building on the baseball diamond, the pole sitting where the boys slid into second base. What a chance the teachers took to plan an outdoor performance! In West Texas any kind of weather can blow in on any day at any season. However, as I remember it, it was an ideal evening. We started our dance early, so we were finished before dark, then moved inside for the remainder of the evening's program. The teachers borrowed benches from the Baptist Church, which stood within arm's reach of the schoolhouse, and arranged them in rows in front of the maypole so the parents could be comfortably seated. At least, they were as comfortable as one can get on bare wooden-slatted benches, built, more than likely, by members of the congregation.

It was a nice setting. The sinking sun cast its rosy rays on the weaving pink and white streamers as we proceeded through our dance, throwing a soft glow around the dancers that added a theatrical illusion. Even the wind cooperated. Instead of whipping the streamers around and out of hands and generally causing chaos, it chose to favor us with a soft gentle caress.

One of the highly anticipated events of the year for the entire community was the play put on by the upper grades at the end of school. Back then it was about the only contact we farm folk had with the theater. There was a moving picture theater in town which showed films regularly and the Harley Sadler tent show came to Post every year for a week of performances but the trip into town was too long for farm families to make after dark. Our theatrical yearnings had to be satisfied with the three-act play the Ragtown pupils produced. The play, a comedy or melodrama, was chosen with care. The parts were assigned to the most talented or the one who could "look" the part. No Helen Hayes or Richard Burton sprung from our ranks, but we watched the performances as avidly as though every actor was a star.

On the night of the play the first thing we saw was the stage curtain. Rolled down, it was in itself entertaining. In the very center, encircled by an ornate, painted-on frame, was the picture of a huge ship tossing on rolling waters and stormy clouds tangled across an angry sky. Since most of us had never seen a ship, much less that much water, it stirred our imaginations to ridiculous heights. Surrounding this work of art were printed advertisements from Post merchants. It was a bonus treat.

In due time the curtain slowly began to rise, its pulley and rollers squeaking and grinding, silencing the noisy crowd, causing a shiver of excitement as it halted at the top and revealed the scene on the stage. The anticipation was as keen as an opening night at any Broadway show.

From the first spoken lines our attention was riveted on the unfolding drama. Before our eyes, the characters, who only that day were the older boys and girls, freckled and tanned, hair in all manner of disarray, in their overalls and print dresses, rough brogans and sturdy oxfords — all so familiar and ordinary — were now strangers with rouged cheeks and lips and hair in unrecognizable arrangements. Their costumes completed the disguise so they lost their identity and became the characters on the stage. We younger kids hung on every word and every movement and could hardly wait to reach upper grades so we could be in the play.

The year I was in the first grade they put on a western play, a very popular theme in our vicinity. All progressed just as anticipated and practiced until the end of the last act when the hero shot the villain, using a real gun loaded with blanks. A murmur went up from the audience as the shot rang out. It was a tense moment. I was totally engrossed, lost in the story so dramatically unfolding before me, so much so that there was no separation in my mind between fact and fiction. Simultaneous with the murmur from the audience, a scream pierced the tense auditorium — mine. I screamed and ran bawling and hollering for my Auntie. This impromptu act drowned out the lines on the stage, diluting to dust the dramatic moment when the hero clasped the heroine to his bosom and planted an impassioned kiss on her lips. This tender scene was forever after to be remembered as anticlimactic. My family, acutely embarrassed, longed to strangle me — and so did ninety-nine percent of the audience. The exceptions were my classmates sharing the front row seats with me, who were much more interested in following my performance than the one taking place on the stage. It is a wonder the hero did not turn his gun on me — loaded with real bullets. No doubt this particular scene had been rehearsed over and over in order to act it out with dramatic perfection, no one ever dreaming a wildly screaming kid would bring all their efforts to such an ignoble end.

A first grader's humiliation is short-lived. I remember Auntie later telling Grandma and Aunt Mattie, who had not attended, "Helen Maude put on the biggest show of all." I was busy playing with my dolls and gave very little attention to what they had to say about it.

The final acts of spring, after crops were planted, were to plow and plant the garden and give the house its annual spring cleaning. School was out so I was available to help with these chores. This is not to say I was pleased with this condition; I would have much preferred to loll around, playing with my dolls, climbing the mulberry tree or indulging in one of the make-up games I played with myself. But farm children knew they were expected to bear their share of the work in proportion to their size and ability and did so without grumbling or argument. A simple announcement — "The garden has to be planted today" — told us all we needed to know. We knew we were expected to report to the garden and be told what job was ours.

The almanac was consulted for the proper planting day. All planting must be done in the right sign of the moon for the plants to grown and produce productively. Once I overheard Auntie and Aunt Mattie discussing Aunt Nancy's beans. "I hope Nancy's beans make. But I doubt they will." "Course they won't. All bush and no beans is what you get when you plant in the light of the moon."

When planting day arrived Uncle hitched one of the mules to a one-row turning plow and plowed the furrows. He walked behind the plow, the harness lines looped around his neck, his hands on the long, curved handles as he guided it up and down the length of the garden, giving gentle commands to the mule. When he had finished plowing the rows, Auntie and I took over.

Auntie walked down a row and with a hoe dug a shallow hole. I followed her with a sack of beans and dropped three in the hole. Auntie, with a skillful turn of the hoe, covered it with soil, moved forward about a foot, dug another hole, I dropped in three beans and thus we moved down the length of the garden. After we planted as many rows as Auntie felt sufficient for summer eating and canning, we planted peas in the same manner — blue hulls, black-eyed, krouder and one short row of English peas. Their large green pods matured early and were short bearing. Just a few messes of this delicacy and the bushes were pulled up and sweet potatoes planted in their place. Tomato, onion and pepper plants were set out in the rows. They had grown from seeds planted in the cold frame early in the spring. After these plants were set out and plenty of hills of cucumbers, cantaloupe, watermelon, okra and other good things were in the ground, we walked down each row with a bucket of water and a dipper, pouring a dipperful on each plant and hill. The watering had to be done in this fashion every day until the plants were large enough to be irrigated.

The planting was just the first step. A garden needed attention all summer long. It must be watered, weeded, and inspected for worms and bugs; after the vegetables started to mature, they must be picked regularly. And the chickens had to be kept out. They liked to fly over the fence to peck the plants and vegetables and scratch up the beds. I was appointed lookout for this eventuality — Old Chill and me, that is. When a hen was imprudent enough to fly over the fence, I'd say to Chill, "Siccum" and he'd sail over the fence and give chase. The hen, put to flight and back in the yard, he'd return from his successful mission, panting and grinning, tongue hanging out the side of his mouth and tail wagging — proud of his victorious mission and rightfully so.

In the depth of summer, early in the morning while the dew was still on, Auntie would come in from the garden with a big milk bucket in one hand and the hem of her apron caught up with the other, both bucket and apron filled with red, ripe tomatoes, green tender cucumbers, snap beans, pearl white onions with soil still clinging on the roots, okra, squash and a luscious cantaloupe, its rough, yellow rind making a bright splash in the array of color dumped on the kitchen sink.

Hand in glove with garden planting was the arrival of baby calves, pigs and rabbits. Once Bonnie had twin calves. What excitement that caused! Neighbors came from all around to see them, for twins born to a cow is an unusual occurrence. They were beautiful. Jersey calves have rich golden coats and huge brown eyes outlined with long black lashes — so cunning, switching their little tails, running and cavorting about the cowpen, coming to an abrupt halt to nuzzle against a little girl or chew on her dress skirt as she stroked its soft coat and felt the buds on the top of the head where horns would eventually grow.

It was fun to count the piglets after the old brood sow delivered. For cuteness a piglet is tough competition. Our hogs were Poland China breed so the progeny were black with a dainty pink nose with which they constantly nudged for a place at their mother's double row of teats. Contrary to the spiny, coarse hairs covering the grown hog's body, piglets' are soft and downy. They are cuddly to hold — if you are brave enough to reach into the pen and pick one up. Mother hogs are not the friendliest of creatures.

Every spring when Uncle was plowing in the field he would come upon a nest of rabbits. The mother, frightened, might spring from the nest; most usually, she would be away looking for food. Uncle would take one of the bunnies and tuck it in his overall pocket. When he finished the round he would leave the team and plow and bring it to the house. He would say to me, "Close your eyes and hold out your hands." In a moment I'd feel an incredibly soft bulk in my hand and, opening my eyes, I'd see a perfect little brown bunny, his heart beating wildly. Folding him close to me, I'd take him inside the house and there he would stay until he was too old and big to be hopping about the house. Our dog respectfully allowed this privilege. We fed them lettuce and carrots from the garden and vegetables left on our plate after a meal. At one time we had one that liked candy, preferring homemade divinity. My bunnies learned to munch popcorn. Wild rabbits make satisfactory pets.

As the days grew warm, buds appeared on the fruit trees. Then all at once, it seemed the whole orchard was in bloom. The fragrance was wonderful. I loved walking between the rows of trees smelling the apple blossoms, then up and down smelling the peach blooms and working my way last of all to my favorite, an old gnarled plum tree which stood at the very end of the plum row. It was more lovely than all the rest. I'd climb onto a low limb and bury my nose into the rich, delicate aroma of its lacy ivory blossoms. With the orchard separating me from all the farm buildings and the house I could settle into a world of fantasy and not come back to earth until I heard Auntie calling, "Helen Maude! Helen Maude!" Then my feet touched the ground.

Spring cleaning. A sacred rite which if not performed would bring on a calamity too awesome to consider. Auntie and Aunt Mattie worked together, first our house, then Grandma and Grandpa's. Cleaning days must be sunny with enough breeze to flap quilts hanging on the line. This was the first act of the first day of cleaning — strip the beds and hang the quilts on the line. Take all the quilts out of the quilt box or off the closet shelves and hang them on the line. They made a rainbow of color — Log Cabin, Nine Patch, Dresden Plate, Wedding Ring, Friendship, Snowball and Butterfly, Flower Basket — flapping back and forth like a flock of exotic birds. At the end of day, smelling of sunshine and fresh breezes, they were restored to the quilt box. All except for one to go on each bed for covering up when summer nights grew chilly.

The bedsprings were lifted from the beds and laid in the front yard on long boards snitched from the lumber pile out back of the barn. The collection of lint and dust was "broomed" from the springs and then they were hosed down. Next the mattresses were moved out and laid on the springs. These were filled with our own carded cotton, or with Aunt Nancy's or Mrs. Childress' duck and geese feathers. All mattresses were given a full day outside, being turned at the half-way point. It was a great temptation to hop into the middle of one and jump up and down. My aunts, however, sternly reminded me they were not to be jumped on.

Only the wooden slats on which the springs rested were left on the stripped beds. These were swept clean and stacked on the front porch.

After quilts and mattresses had their day in the sun, the beds were reassembled and made up with summer sheets, starched and ironed pillowcases and the good smelling quilts. When we went to bed that night and slipped between the sheets we had the same sensation as when we'd changed from black ribbed stockings to knee socks.

While the sun and air were doing their good work, plenty was going on inside the house. The curtains were removed from the windows, taken outside for a good shaking or thrown into a tub of suds to be washed. The windows were cleaned until they sparkled, the facings and frames wiped down. Baseboards around the room were wiped with furniture polish. A clean cloth was tied over the broom and it was used to sweep down ceilings and walls. These preliminaries finished, it was time for the star performance of spring cleaning — scouring the floors. In other parts of the country women scrubbed floors but in West Texas we scoured ours.

For this important operation a large bucket of hot sudsy water was set in the middle of the room. The aunts dipped in their brooms bringing them out full of the suds and began to scrub, working from the center toward the walls. When every square inch of the floor had been scoured to their satisfaction the suds bucket was filled with clear water and switched over the room. With their brooms they pushed and swept the water through the outside doors. By mid-afternoon, with air circulating through the open windows and doors, the floors were dry enough to move the furniture back in place once each piece had been polished front, back and underneath.

The cleaning was done systematically room by room. I don't know how many days it took to complete both houses, but the results proved the adage, "cleanliness is next to godliness," for "heavenly" is the only way to describe the feeling at the end of spring cleaning. Proudly we inspected spick-and-span windows, the mellow glow of polished woodwork and the patina of creamy yellow pine floors. Now we could face summer in good order.

Earlier in the spring, before plowing and planting time, men did their own spring cleaning. The chicken-house floor had to be cleaned of all droppings, the roosts must be swept clean and the cow barn had to cleaned. With a short-handled scoop, the manure that had collected through the winter months was thrown onto a wagonbed and hauled to an area in the field that needed to be fertilized. The barnyards were similarly cleansed and distributed. For these undertakings Uncle put on his knee-high rubber boots and his oldest work clothes so that when he finished with these messy, dirty, smelly jobs he could wash off his boots at the yard faucet. If Auntie couldn't bear to wash his clothes, she could throw them in the trash. The water trough where the cows, mules and horses drank had to be drained, scrubbed clean, and refilled from the storage tank. Farm equipment had to be inspected to make sure it was in good order — a general checking up to see if winter had inflicted any damage that had to be corrected before the busy season began.

Of course, the boys in the family were pressed into helping with these unsavory duties just as the girls were required to help with spring-cleaning the house.

Short-sleeved dresses and knee socks, shirt sleeves instead of cumbersome sweaters, warm sun and gentle wind, bird songs, fresh planted fields and no school were realities that created a lighthearted aura over the land — life was almost unbearably good.

SUMMER

When considering my growing-up years, squinting my eyes through the cobwebby dust of those far-off days of the 1920s, it seems that summer held the very essence of life — the kind of days you can look back on and say, "Those were the good old days."

It was the season for an assortment of good things we did not experience at any other time of year. Eating was a prominent feature, our table groaning under an abundance of fried chicken, ice cream, leaf lettuce, fried okra, watermelon, cantaloupe and other good foods that were strictly summer fare. It meant kinfolk coming to visit and making pal-

lets on the floor for cousins to sleep on and turn somersaults. It was going barefoot and the Fourth of July county picnic at Two Draw Lake. It was seeing our flat, barren,
brown plains turn into one vast, green carpet as cotton
and row crops covered the fields and cow pastures were
lush with native grass.

June was the honeymoon month in every sense of the
word. Its warm, gentle breeze moved through the open
windows and doors. The flowers in the front yard gave off
their fragrance, the blooming yellow rose bushes opened
their first blossoms. A line of zinnias planted beside the
front walk was full of colorful blooms, the bed of sweet-
peas and cosmos spread their delicate aroma across the
yard, and the row of locust trees marching down the west
side of the house were a mass of creamy, waxy blooms,
their perfume mixing with all the other good smells of
summer. The petals, when pulled from the stem and
opened up, produced a single drop of nectar so delicious
it is impossible to find anything comparable to describe it.

The mulberry tree was full of fruit. I'd climb high up
into its branches to a comfortable perch and there I'd sit
(sometimes with a friend or cousin), gorging myself on
the sickly sweet berries. Climbing down, hands, lips and
garments stained purple from the berries, I was ready for
the inevitable scolding from Auntie. It was a persistent,
stubborn stain almost impossible to wash out of a garment
and requiring several scrubbings with soap and water to
get it off of face and hands. No wonder Auntie was ready
to cut a switch from the nearest peach tree. I wonder that
she didn't.

The bright refreshing green of the vegetable gardens,
orchards and trees — like a fairyland unfolding after the
long, drab days of fall and winter — gave June its special

mystique. School, faded and forgotten, summer lay ahead with its carefree days stretching away into the distance.

Granny Bailey, no relation, was a colorful, snuff-dipping family friend of long-standing. She came every summer and stayed two or three weeks (which never seemed long enough for any of us) and entertained us with her spicy philosophy and tales about her family and friends. As she embroidered these tales, she stopped from time to time, holding us in suspense while she disposed a glob of snuffy spit into the tin can I'd been commissioned to fill with dirt and place beside her chair. I don't think I ever saw her frown. Even when she told us, in graphic detail, about her son Tobe's barn burning she had an aura of pleased excitement about her. She described the horrifying sparks that soared above the house, the frantic evacuation of the frightened farm animals and the futile tears of Tobe's wife. She ended this absorbing report by saying, "And I told Tobe — Tobe, I said, trouble comes in threes so get ready!" Then, over her steel-rimmed spectacles, she looked straight into my eyes and said, "Remember that, child. Trouble comes in threes."

I did remember it; it hovered uneasily on the rim of my mind and came forcibly into focus on a dismal day in June when all our cats were shot, lodging there, an ominous threat of doom.

Auntie and Uncle decided to try their luck with a new enterprise to bring more cash money into the family coffers — raising turkeys for the Thanksgiving and Christmas market. They had no previous experience raising turkeys, but the young, enthusiastic county agent came to the farm, told them all he knew, which was what he had learned in his college class, and left a handful of illustrated brochures lying on the library table for them to study. They spent many winter evenings poring over these brochures and figuring, excitedly, with pencil and tablet how much money they could reasonably expect to make from what, by now, they were convinced was a no-fail project.

Turkeys, it seems, love to roam and are not particular whose property they roam on. Having no special fences or barriers to keep them on the home place they were a considerable nuisance to our neighbors and for this reason an embarrassment to Uncle.

They were irresponsible parents with very little concern for what happened to the poults once they were hatched and able to go about. Our cats had more interest in them than the parents. Normally, cats are not aggressive with farm denizens but this was a new species and one that seemed not too smart nor too protected. They soon found they could pounce on a defenseless, cheeping poult and maul it around, tear off a wing, attack its neck in which case it would bleed to death and, at times, one could very well serve as a meal.

Uncle and Auntie were at their wit's end to know how to stop this daily carnage. They tried every deterrent they could think of or that anyone suggested, but nothing seemed to work. The county agent was no help; there had been nothing in his textbook about cats who had an appetite for young, tender turkey. The hard, cold facts were, however, that every time a cat killed or maimed one of the helpless little turkeys he was taking money out of our family pocket. Finally, as a drastic measure to rescue what they could of their investment, they decided the cats would have to go. No other farm family would be willing to take five cats with such a bad reputation, so the only alternative was to shoot them.

Grandpa volunteered to help Uncle with this unsavory chore and arrived on the appointed day with gun in hand. It was uncharacteristic for either Grandpa or Uncle to be seen in such a role and I did not blame them for what must be done. When a farm animal goes bad it must be gotten rid of.

Yet, knowing this did not keep me from feeling it was the worst kind of tragedy. I remember lying on my bed that violent, bruising day with my hands over my ears so I could not hear the gunshots as they rounded up and killed the cats. I did not hear the wheels of the wagon as they hauled them down the lane and to the cow pasture to bury the bodies. Only our old mama cat was spared; her five robust, half-grown sons and daughters were dead. I sobbed until I could not talk coherently. These cats were pets and, although I understood why they must go, the anguish and pain and sadness was almost unbearable.

After this shattering experience not a day passed I did not remember Granny Bailey's admonition. An uneasy dread followed me like a shadow as one summer day followed the other and I waited for another fateful blow to fall.

The first day it was really warm and all traces of spring chill had disappeared, permission was given to shoe-weary kids to run barefoot. How good it felt! At first every little clod of dirt was painful to our tender feet but before many days had passed the soles of our feet were toughened and we could race around with great abandon.

There were, mercifully, few rocks or stones in West Texas. Gravel had to be brought into the chicken yard for the hens and roosters and was the nearest thing to rocks we saw except the chalky ones in Yellow House Canyon. Gravel was a necessary ingredient for chicken craws where the mastication of their food took place and occasionally stray pebbles from the gravel pile were found in the yard proper; if we stepped down on one of these we'd get a painful stone bruise.

A bandaged toe was not uncommon, either, for there were all manner of places or things that could cause one to stub a toe. However, these hazards were willingly borne for the privilege of going barefoot.

For pure ecstasy nothing could compare with scrunching around one's bare feet in an old hen's dirt bath. The hen, feeling the need for a good cleansing, prepared herself a bath. Selecting a spot near a fence row where the dirt was soft and using her long yellow claws, she scratched out a bowl-shaped indentation in the ground, working the dirt with her feet until it was as smooth as talcum powder. Preparations complete, according to her satisfaction, she sat in the "bowl" and using her feet and wings, threw the dirt up over her body, under her wings, wiggling and squirming to get every part of her body "washed" with the soft dirt. When she considered herself to be thoroughly cleansed she stood up, stretched her wings and shook herself, a shower of dust filling the air about her. Happy with her clean body, she walked away singing in that incomparable way that only a hen can sing. The bath would be used by other members of the flock. It was also used by barefoot boys and girls. It did not clean the feet but the soft dirt working around the toes and the soles of the feet was closely akin to a spiritual experience.

In direct contrast to the ecstasy of going barefoot was the plague of summer — wearing a sun bonnet. This was an encumbrance visited on girls only; boys wore straw hats. Bonnets were hot and the wind flopped them across one's face so a person couldn't see — a nuisance; something else to keep washed, starched and ironed. Regardless of the inconvenience, however, no self-respecting female would go out into the summer sun without first tying a sunbonnet on her head. Suntan, in the '20s was not considered beautiful nor desirable. Freckles, the bane of the fair-skinned girl, was even more to be deplored than tan skin.

Two big-selling items at the drugstores were freckle cream and bleaching cream. Freckle cream, when properly applied to the face, faded the freckles sufficiently so they could be well concealed with other cosmetics. Bleaching cream caused the tan layer of skin to peel off, leaving a soft white complexion. It did, that is, if it were evenly applied; if not, it could leave the face in a peculiar condition of white and tan splotches.

My bonnet hung on a knob behind the kitchen door along with Auntie's and with Uncle's wide-brimmed straw hat. When I played in the shade of the house or a tree I could take off the bonnet, but how is a little girl to remember, or take the trouble, to tie it on again when she only wants to run to the next tree or inside the house to get a doll dress she forgot or to investigate an interesting bug crawling across the yard? At the beginning of summer it was like a refrain, "Helen Maude! Put your bonnet on and keep it on!" This continued until I had transgressed so often that I was as tan as my little Mexican friend who came in the fall to pick our cotton. But all my friends were also tan or freckled. The battle of the bonnet went on in all households and was similarly lost.

Located in the north window of the kitchen was the

all-important window cooler. June was the month to put it into service. It was a wooden lean-to about forty inches square built over the lower half of the window, completely covering the opening and resting on stilts. The roof was slanted to turn water and the three exposed sides were screened. On the floor inside the enclosure was placed a shallow metal pan about three inches deep and as square wide as the window opening. The pan was filled halfway up with water and the butter, milk, cream and other perishables were placed in it. A wet cloth covered the food and extended on all sides into the water. As the wind circulated through the screen, blowing on the wet cloth (which was constantly absorbing more water from the pan so that it was always wet) the food was kept sufficiently cool to keep from spoiling.

Our cooler was just beside the back door and the slanted roof was a handy place to set things, for the time being, that were meant to go inside. Uncle would leave the hammer or screwdriver there when he didn't want to take trouble to put them away in the toolbox which sat under the north window in the back bedroom. Auntie would toss her gardening gloves up there when she wasn't ready to go inside. I left numerous things there — the book I'd been reading under the apple tree, my bonnet, my mud pie utensils and one hot July evening I left my favorite doll on the roof overnight. She was a "mama" doll and her name was Betty. She had a large, soft, cuddly body — a generous armful, a composition head, feet and hands, and eyes that opened and closed. I dressed and undressed her many times a day, rocked her to sleep, swung her in my swing and talked to her. I loved her.

That night, accompanied by a frightening display of lightning and thunder, it came a torrential rainstorm, the kind that, on rare occasions, a hot July day can produce. The next morning I rushed to the door to look out and see the clean-washed sky and the puddles of water standing in the backyard. Instead my eyes were drawn to the strange-looking, water-soaked object that had once been my beloved Betty. Her composition face was cracked and pealed, and her stuffed body was a soggy, deformed, unidentifiable mass, her eyes gazing crazily sideways. I could not believe what I was seeing; it must be I was still in bed and this was a bad, bad dream. But I was awake for above me a few white puffy clouds were floating across a crisp, blue sky and the yard was dotted with puddles of water. Old Chill was wagging his tail and nuzzling my hand. Then with a sickening stab Granny Bailey's piercing look and doom-filled words flashed into my mind: "Trouble comes in threes." First the cats and now Betty — one more still to go. All day long, in a state of shock and grief over my monumental loss, I battled the inevitability of another tragedy and the fear of not knowing when it would strike nor what it would be.

For years the window cooler was the only icebox we had. Then one day the real thing made its appearance in our kitchen and in so doing created for me a new and despicable chore — emptying the drip pan. Constructed of wood, stained and varnished to look like a piece of furniture, with shiny metal handles that were works of art, these iceboxes are now sold for a considerable price in antique stores. Our box opened from the top to take the block of ice; the space beneath was lined in metal where the food was stored, and beneath and below everything was the receptacle for the melted ice — the drip pan. It was shallow, unwieldy and designed to try the patience of a saint. Removing one that was full of water presented test after test. First, it must be pulled from beneath the icebox without spilling water over the sides. Next, it must be ever so carefully lifted from the floor. The real test, then, was to walk with it balanced in one's hands to the kitchen sink and dump it without spilling and sloshing water all over the floor. I seldom passed even one test and never all of them.

The icebox was a vast improvement over the window cooler though not so inexpensive for it required that we buy ice. The iceman made his rural route twice a week. So he would know how much to leave us, we were supplied with a cardboard that had four selections printed in large black numbers: 100 on one side with an upside-down 75; 50 on the other with an upside-down 25. We propped this in the front window with the proper number upright. If it was not in the window when the iceman came by, he drove on to the next customer. If there was a delivery to be made, he came to the back door calling out "Iceman," a leather apron across his back where the block of ice rested in the clutches of a huge iron tong, with which he maneuvered the ice into its proper place in the top of the box. It was clearly understood that this block of ice was for keeping the box cold and not to chip pieces for iced tea or ice cream or to chomp.

As in all other seasons, the wind and weather played special roles. We seldom had a sandstorm in summer but we had other conditions of discomfort to deal with.

Come July the sun was a considerable factor, beating down relentlessly day after day, joining forces with the wind to assault us with a dry, searing heat that parched our skin, burned our eyes and bare feet as we walked on the hard, baked ground. It withered the gardens and crops if it persisted long enough, forcing rugged farmers to their knees to pray for rain. The animals, during these spells, grew nervous and cross. The chickens hovered in any shade they could find, panting through their open beaks. If the dry heat extended over a period of days it could cause great destruction.

A favorite trick of summer wind was to die down and not blow at all — not even enough to move a leaf on the mulberry tree. This would occur during late July or in August when the sun was at its zenith. Our biggest worry was whether there would be enough water in the storage tank to water the stock, for if there was not enough wind to turn the windmill no water could be pumped to replace what was rapidly disappearing from the tank. The lower the water level dropped the greater the tension grew; not a drop of water could be wasted. At these times we were willing to take the wind in any form we could get it. These were the hottest days of all; even the hot winds were preferable to this stifling heat. Devious and provoking, the wind seemed to be hiding in some secret place, chuckling at our discomfort and anxiety.

On such summer evenings, after supper, Auntie, Uncle and I would sit on the front porch until the house cooled down enough to go to bed. Sometimes neighbors would walk over and sit with us, leaving while there was still enough twilight to light their way home. When it was finally bedtime, the air inside the house had cooled down but the bedsheets were still hot. Sleep came slowly, and lying in the stillness I could hear every night sound, the mules and cows shifting around in their lots, the dog moving from porch to yard and back to the porch again looking for a cool spot. In the distance a dog barked or howled, and one on a neighboring farm answered. Old Chill would rouse himself and put in a polite bark or two.

Then abruptly cutting through the peaceful night, seducing all my senses, could be heard the distant chug-chug of a freight train and its long mournful whistle as it rolled into Yellow House Canyon over eight miles away, a sound that penetrated emotions I could not identify. A bittersweet nostalgia constricted my throat as I lay listening to the long, haunting notes piercing the night, hanging like an echo across the miles, splintering my imagination into a burst of stars and leaving me with a lonesome, unexplainable longing. Heat and discomfort were forgotten as my emotions wandered through this delightful and disturbing summer experience, straining my ears to hear the last fading sounds as the train sped across the plains and into the canyon on its journey through the night.

As the night progressed the heat became less and less until by midnight I woke up enough to pull up a sheet; before morning I was reaching sleepily for a quilt.

Another wind activity peculiar to summer was the whirlwind. A wisp of wind dipped down onto the ground, picked up dust, then began whirling it around in corkscrew fashion, picking up more dust as it whirled, gaining momentum until it developed into a whirling dervish of wind and sand extending in a thin, high spiral into the sky. It moved swiftly across fields and farmyards and across barns and houses, through open windows scattering papers, blowing handmade dresser scarves across the room and roughing up the window curtains. If clothes were hanging outside on the line they were twisted together in an impossible tangle. A whirlwind developed so quickly there was no way to prepare for one. If you were caught out in one it was difficult to stand up against its force. It was a menace, but it dissipated as quickly and mysteriously as it formed, leaving us to straighten out its mischief.

Even with the discomfort of hot wind, stifling stillness and whirlwinds, there were many compensations to summer that far outweighed these discomforts. It was a paradox, summer was, for there were many long, hard days of work from sunup to sundown and many long, lazy glorious days of idle freedom. These days of freedom meant there were no restrictions. We farm kids could daydream, play, visit neighbor kids, spend time alone, and sometimes, in the tediously slow passing of time, be bored. On those days by ten o'clock in the morning we were asking every fifteen minutes if it wasn't time for dinner. The afternoon seemed to go on forever, as if the earth had ceased to revolve, leaving the sun stuck in the sky halfway between noon and sunset. Contrarily, however, most summer days were savored to the last fading twilight moments.

My favorite spot for a long, carefree summer day was in the orchard under the boughs of the farthest apple tree. Undisturbed, I let my mind wander to investigate curiosities, mysteries and puzzling questions. It was a time to watch idly as a doodlebug made its ponderous way across the yard only to suddenly eject its wings and fly away; listen to the monotonous buzz of a wasp; watch a scissortail balance itself on the telephone wire, spreading and closing the two long feathers that made up its tail; look into the endless horizon and wonder what lay beyond. It was the best of all times to curl up with a book and read to its end, without stopping. And to play make-believe — the best of creative imagining. These days belonged individually to each child. "Sweet childish days, that were as long as twenty days are now," wrote Wordsworth. How well he knew those summers of long ago.

There was more work to be done in summer than any other season. Field work was a constant, unending job and, as with all other farm jobs, the children were expected to do their share. Girls were not excused from field work except when it was necessary to help with household chores.

Hoeing was inevitable and unavoidable. Weeds that grew in the rows and in and around the plants were hoed out. We walked up and down the rows pulling out weeds by the roots with the sharp edge of the hoe or cutting them off even with the ground, being careful not to disturb or cut down the cotton plants or small tender shoots of the feed crop.

Auntie always helped Uncle hoe the crop. Though Uncle was a good farmer and we had a minimum of weeds in the field, he felt the same about weeds as he did about crooked rows — not to be tolerated — so we usually went over the crop twice during the growing season. It took about two weeks to go over the entire field, walking from sunup to sundown.

When I was very small Uncle improvised a tent in the turn row, at the end of the rows where they were hoeing, to shelter me from the wind and sun. He drove a couple of poles into the ground, laid a crossbar across them and draped a piece of ducking over all, staking it so the wind wouldn't blow it off. I had my doll to play with, a quilt to sit or lie on and Old Chill for companionship and protection. He performed this assignment vigilantly and patiently. The water jug, once a glass vinegar container, was placed in the shade of my tent. Auntie had covered the outside with a tow sack and sewed it securely in place. This wrapping was soaked with water and, in the shade with the wind blowing, it kept the water inside the jug nice and cool. In the intense heat a drink at the end of a round was necessary. Only the constant blowing of the west wind kept the sun from being unendurable to Auntie and Uncle as they walked the long, half-mile rows — a full mile every round.

When I was a little bigger (we were judged more by size than by age) Uncle made a short-handled hoe for me. I still had the tent but I walked rounds with them from time to time, hoeing weeds on their rows, getting in their way, but feeling my importance at sharing in real farm work. It was fun. It ceased to be fun when I was older and big enough to handle a regular hoe and was expected to carry my own row right along with my parents. When Uncle would announce at the supper table that we would "hoe the crop" beginning "in the morning" my heart sank. There were many more interesting things to do than bundle up in work clothes and walk up and down cotton rows in the blazing July sun. I dreaded going to bed that night, for it meant we had to get up next morning and go to the field.

We dressed for field work, Auntie and I, even when I carried my little hoe. A "stay" bonnet was of foremost importance. Stays — lengths of cardboard cut about two inches wide and the length of the bonnet — were slipped into gussets sewn into the bonnet. The "skirt" of the bonnet hung over the sides and back of the neck. Most farm women wore this type of bonnet to do outdoor chores and to work in the field. There was such a thing as a housedress in those days, made of gingham from a plain sensible pattern for easy washing and ironing. Auntie, Aunt Mattie and Grandma had a collection of these, as did all farm women, and this is what they wore to do housework and chores. For the field Auntie and I each wore one of these dresses that was too old and faded for any other use. Stockings with the feet cut out were pulled up over our arms and fastened with safety pins at the shoulders of the dress. Canvas gloves completed the ensemble. Dressed in this fashion, our arms, hands, neck and face were protected from the sun. Auntie powdered her face before she went to the field. She said it made her feel like a lady while doing man's work.

The garden produced its bounty of vegetables and what was not consumed for daily summer meals was canned or preserved. When canning days were announced, kids abandoned all hope of getting to play and resigned themselves to a long, tedious, unbroken workday.

Vegetables had to be picked early in the morning while they were at the peak of freshness. They were picked, washed and prepared in whatever way was appropriate. Green beans were snapped, peas shelled, tomatoes dipped in scalding water and skinned, okra sliced for gumbo, cucumbers set in brine to pickle, green tomatoes, pepper and onions chopped for chow-chow relish. As the fruit in the orchard ripened what was not eaten right off the trees was canned, preserved or made into jelly. Preserve- and jelly-making was a necessary part of "putting up" fruit, for whoever had heard of eating hot biscuits — a staple at most farm breakfast tables — without heaping on jelly or preserves? And pickled peaches — one of the best of the goodies which Auntie served as a side dish at a Sunday dinner or for special occasions. Creating this storehouse of food meant many backbreaking hours in the kitchen where huge steaming pots of water and sputtering pressure cookers heated the kitchen to an unbearably high temperature.

I think I must have been more useful on canning days than at any other time. I fetched empty glass jars from the cellar, complaining that my knees and legs were ready to drop off from climbing up and down the cellar steps; I helped pick vegetables and fruit, sure that my arms would drop off and my back break; I shelled peas and snapped beans until my fingers were numb. Yet, the instant I was told I was not needed any longer, all my aches and pains miraculously disappeared and I went frolicking out to play until darkness drove me inside.

On canning day early in the morning while the dew was still on the ground I'd go with Auntie and we'd pick buckets full of black-eyed peas. We brought them in the house and dumped them on a quilt spread on the floor in the front room. Unless otherwise occupied in the kitchen where the actual canning process went on, all hands, including Uncle's and Grandpa's (if they were not busy in the fields), would be seated around the mound of peas, a pan between their knees and fingers, busily shelling. It was such a discouragingly huge pile that I was sure we'd be shelling all day, but by noon we could see the quilt. Hope rose to replace despair — there would be some playtime left in the day after all.

Sometimes aunts and cousins would be present to help — then we cousins would make a game of it. We'd turn hide-the-thimble into a guessing game. I would think of a hiding place and the others had to guess where the thimble was hidden instead of searching for it in the usual way. We made up one game in which each person around the circle must think of a fruit, vegetable or animal, beginning with a letter in the alphabet, taken in order, while someone counted to ten. If you could not name one beginning with your letter you were out of the game. Our favorite was building a story. One person started the story, the next person in the circle added to the plot and so on around the circle. This would go on until we tired of the story or it found a logical conclusion. Using our ingenuity in this way, we made a dull job lively and finished it much more quickly.

Fried chicken was one of those delicious delicacies that made summer special. Fried chicken had its beginning when the first warm days of spring put thoughts of motherhood into the farmyard hens. A hen indicated her desire for fulfillment by setting. She would find a nest where several hens had laid eggs, and, hovering over them, she would refuse to leave the nest. Gathering the eggs that had been laid that day was my evening chore and I dreaded doing it when we began to have setting hens. Not only would the hen refuse to get off the nest but neither would she allow me to reach under her to pick up the eggs. When I would attempt to do either she ruffed her feathers, lay back her comb and pecked at me with her very solid beak. No one knows what pain is until they have been pecked by a setting hen.

We had brooder houses which were especially built for the hens and their baby chicks. These houses were very small, built to accommodate only one hen and her brood. A wooden box filled with hay or cottonseed was placed in the back of the house to receive the eggs. After dark set in and kerosene lamps were lit in the house, Auntie would select twelve or thirteen of the nicest-looking eggs, most uniform in size, and bring them to the kitchen table where the all-important candling took place. Auntie rolled up a sheet of paper to look like a telescope. She held an egg at one end of the paper, close to the chimney of the lighted lamp, and the other end of the paper to her eye. This made it possible to see through the thin shell and search for the telltale small knot clinging to the yolk. If the knot was present it meant the egg was fertile and would produce a baby chick. After all the eggs had been put to the test and found acceptable, she carried them out to the brooder house and carefully placed them in the prepared nest. With gloves on to protect her hands from the ever-ready beak, she gently lifted the setting hen off her temporary nest, tucked the hen's head under her arm, transported her to the new nest and set her upon the eggs. The hen, indignant over being disturbed and moved about, expressed her displeasure by quarreling and ruffing her neck feathers and at once set to work rearranging the nest to her own specifications. This accomplished, she moved the eggs about until the arrangement pleased her, settled down upon them and, with a few throaty clucks, dismissed us. We could leave her to carry out her mission, making sure she always had sufficient water and feed inside the little chicken-wire fence that enclosed her domain.

The chicks were yellow and downy and fun to hold in one's hand. I often took one for a pet. I once had a pet rooster which, after he learned to crow, would come to the back door of the house and crow and keep crowing until I came outside and hand-fed him.

The fluffy, yellow chicks of springtime became the pullets and young roosters of summertime, sending Auntie, Uncle and me on our annual search for the chicken hook, a long, sturdy piece of heavy wire, crooked at one end. The hook fit around the leg of an unsuspecting young rooster (pullets never reached the frying pan — they were meant to grow up and lay eggs), and when he felt the wire touch his leg, he was startled into making a dash for freedom which caused the hook to catch his foot and thus seal his doom. What we usually did was throw out a pan of grain and when the eager youngsters gathered for the feast, select the most likely candidate and pull him in.

A kettle of scalding hot water was waiting for him as soon as Auntie wrung his neck. A cruel thing to do, I suppose, but we never thought of it that way since roosters were raised to be eaten. Auntie grasped the victim's head firmly in her hand, swung him over and under a few times until his neck was broken, dropped him on the ground to flop around until she was sure he was dead, then doused him up and down in the bucket of hot water, plucked off his feathers and laid his denuded body in a pan of cold water to draw out the body heat. The bird then was disemboweled and cut up into proper pieces — two wings, two legs, two thighs, a pulley bone, two half breasts, the bony back, the back proper, the liver and the gizzard. These pieces were dipped into a bowl of milk, rolled in flour and dropped into a black iron skillet filled halfway up with hot melted lard. The stove burner was turned down to just right for frying and each piece was turned at the proper moment so that after awhile there appeared on the table golden brown, tender pieces fit for a king.

One of the highlights of summer was making ice cream. This required a trip into town, eight miles away, below the Caprock.

I can't remember ever going to town during those days of the '20s on any day except Saturday. It was the day all farmers went to town. We did not always go in the fall when crops were being gathered nor in the winter when it was cold nor spring when there were sandstorms and surprise blizzards, but in the summer we never missed a Saturday — another star in summer's crown.

The list of supplies we would need to purchase was written down and at the top of the list was "100 lbs. ice." The last thing we did before we left town was drive by Jones Ice House and purchase our ice. A quilt lay ready to wrap the precious cargo. It was securely folded around the block of ice, then tied with binder twine and placed between the back and front seats of our Model-T Ford.

As soon as we got home the ice cream freezer was brought from the pantry and the delightful chore began. Auntie prepared the mixture using plenty of fresh-laid eggs, rich milk and thick cream mixed in with the vanilla flavoring and sugar and whatever else was in her recipe. Uncle layered the salt and ice in the wooden freezer bucket around the can, the mixture was poured into it and the top securely clamped on. An old quilt piece was folded on top for me to sit on to hold the freezer steady while Uncle turned the crank — the real purpose being to keep me occupied and my excitement in hand while it was freezing.

It seemed forever before Uncle would say, "It's getting hard to turn; must be getting done." He would keep turning, though, until it was impossible to make the crank go another turn. Then it had to sit awhile, wrapped with the quilt, to be just the right firmness. Finally, off came the quilt and the can was lifted out of the ice and salt and moved to the kitchen sink to be opened. Auntie removed the dasher, handed it to me on a plate, saying, "Lick the dasher!" How good it tasted — nectar, pure nectar!

Most usually Grandpa, Grandma and Aunt Mattie

would drive over from their farm, two miles away, and enjoy the treat with us, for we had stopped by their house on the way home from town to tell them ice cream would soon be ready to eat. Grandpa loved it; it made him cough but he ate more than anyone. We had as many bowls as we wanted except on the rare occasions when Uncle Baltie, Aunt Flossie and my cousins showed up. Uncle Baltie would spy the freezer sitting temptingly in its quilt, laugh gleefully and say, "Ah-ha! I knew it! I smelled it." Sometimes when I had said my prayers and Auntie had gone from the room and closed my bedroom door, I would pop out of bed and drop on my knees to add a P.S., "Please, God, next time we make ice cream, stop up Uncle Baltie's nose."

The hundred pounds of ice would furnish another weekend delicacy — iced tea. This was almost as special as ice cream. There would be enough ice left, if carefully wrapped and placed in a washtub and pushed into a corner out of the sun, to have tea Saturday for supper and for Sunday dinner and supper. Tea has never tasted so good as it did then, laced with a generous slice of lemon and plenty of sugar. We did not know about dieting or the damaging effects of sugar — whether food tasted good was our main concern.

Getting chunks of ice to eat was another treat. When the ice was being chipped for the tea glasses I could ask one of the aunts for a chunk to suck on and to chomp. If cousins were present many arguments took place over who had been favored with the biggest piece; angry words and hurt feelings sometime resulted from a thoughtless aunt handing out uneven pieces of ice.

I cannot remember ever having ice cream and iced tea any other time of year. We savored every bite and every swallow of food which was only summertime fare. I cannot remember ever wishing for, or thinking about, fried chicken, watermelon, okra and other summer foods after August thirty-first — the cutoff date for summer.

The Garza County Fourth of July picnic at Two Draw Lake was perhaps the most important celebration of the year. Those farmers and ranchers of the '20s, who had come out less than two decades earlier to settle this land, were fiercely devoted to their country. It was unthinkable, traitorous even, to stay away from the celebration for anything less serious than sickness, death or accident. No farm or ranch work was more important on the Fourth of July than attending this event. Likewise, no place of business was open on the Fourth. It would have shown shocking disrespect toward flag and country to have carried on business as if it were an ordinary day.

Patriotism in the 1920s was a vital ingredient in the lives of all of us. We were taught in school and at home to honor, love and appreciate our country. The great giants of history — Washington, Adams, Jefferson, Henry Clay, Lincoln, Paul Revere — were our true heroes. The Constitution, the Declaration of Independence, Betsy Ross and the making of the flag, Francis Scott Key and the "Star Spangled Banner" were thrilling testimonies to the greatness of our country, the very thought of which swelled our hearts with pride and dedication.

The flag symbolized the essence of our patriotism. There was a mystique about Old Glory that could not be put into words; it could only be felt with the heart. It was the bloodshed of the Revolution, Bunker Hill, the Boston Tea Party, the Doughboys of World War I, the brave heroes of the Alamo; it was "government of the people, by the people, for the people," "liberty and justice for all" — sacred trusts we were willing and ready to fight to preserve. To die for one's country was the ultimate heroic sacrifice that a schoolchild of the '20s could envision.

So we celebrated, every able-bodied citizen in the county from the youngest to the oldest. There was a parade, a band and a speech. The parade marched down Main Street in front of an improvised platform where the town dignitaries were seated and where the speech was delivered. After the whooping and cheering, with the last notes of "Stars and Stripes Forever," pumped out by a sweating band, still ringing in our ears, we began the slow, dusty procession up the road that ran north of Post to Two Draw Lake. There would be Model-T Fords, Chevrolets and a few big fancy cars with little flags attached to the radiator ornaments, some horseback riders, and a few horse-drawn vehicles making up the procession. Turning into the grounds, the first thing we saw was the tall flagpole and the flag unfurled in the brisk wind. Beyond, the concessionaires were busily hawking their wares — balloons, sparklers, cotton candy, popcorn, Cracker Jacks, soda pop, ice cream cones and trinkets of various kinds.

Two Draw Lake was the site where most big county celebrations were held. Its source of water was God-knows-where. As seldom as it rained, the lake was no less than phenomenal. The water was often stagnant and green, with slimy algae clinging to its banks. A finger extended out from the main body of the lake, and this is where the activities took place. By some unknown process, the water was reasonably clean in that area. Willow and cottonwood trees grew on the banks around the perimeter of this part of the lake, and a narrow wooden footbridge crossed from west to east, ending by the bathhouse.

The bathhouse was a sturdy, unpainted building. At water level there were two dressing rooms, one for men and one for women. A ramp extended from the bathhouse out over the water; at the end was a diving board and a platform for the lifeguard. Bathers would sit on the ramp and dangle their feet in the water. Above the dressing rooms and the docks was an open deck reached by an outside stairway, which we country kids had fun running up and down. From up there we could see most of the lake and look down on the swimmers below.

Some of my friends went swimming. Lucile and Irene always went in, wearing one of the rented suits. These were made from black knit fabric and styled so the suit began high enough on the body to adequately cover the shoulders and bosom and extended straight down the body to well below the upper thighs. It was a garment designed to protect the bather's "modesty" and discourage ogling from the male population. The men's suits were two-piece, the top designed like a summer undershirt and the trunks reaching almost to their knees. It was entertaining to watch them dive and swim and cavort in the water but I had no desire to join them. In fact, I did not want to go too near the banks, and it took all the courage I could muster to walk across the footbridge. With carefully concealed nervousness I braved this ordeal dozens of times during the day since a good part of our entertainment was walking back and forth across the bridge.

As soon as we arrived at the lake and were parked, I was out of the car searching for my friends and schoolmates — Odie, Irene, Lucile and others. Soon several of us were together and the fun began. First thing we did was head across the bridge to the concessions, clutching our nickels and dimes, avidly discussing what we would buy. Most everyone bought a balloon — one cost a nickel — and extended the pleasure of the purchase by careful consideration of the color. I bought the same thing every year: a small rubber ball, about two inches in diameter, with a long rubber band attached. If you held the end of the band and tossed out the ball the rubber band stretched far away and then sprung back to be caught. I thought it was a wonderful toy and dreamed of owning one for days before the Fourth, for it was the only place I ever saw one for sale. Soda pop was a popular item. Since we had few opportunities to drink soda pop, our palates were not sated from an overabundance of such luxuries and we savored every taste. Delaware Punch was a favorite — purple, grape-flavored and with plenty of fizz. Cotton candy was a must. Its sticky, pink froth got into our windblown hair, all over our faces and on each other. By the time we were finished eating our cones we were a mess and headed for the water faucet that stood by the bathhouse. By this time there was a loblolly around the faucet so we got our shoes wet and muddy while we washed our hands and as we leaned over to hold our mouth under the stream of water, splashing our dresses and socks. We were little concerned how we looked and, anyway, the wind and sun would soon dry us out.

By general consent, when the sun reached the top of the sky folks commenced gathering at their appointed picnic spots. Most everyone found a place under the shade of the willow and cottonwood trees to lay out their picnic spread. And what a great picnic it was!

Farm women put to use all manner of containers to transport their picnic food — washtubs, buckets, boxes, milk cans and one Fourth a family parked near us brought their food in a trunk. I could not keep my eyes away as the mother brought out dish after dish from the seemingly bottomless trunk. Our two wooden boxes — one had held prunes and one apples — which we used year after year to pack our food made a poor showing compared to such a glamorous container.

Uncle and Grandpa took the boxes from the car while Auntie and Aunt Mattie spread a quilt on the ground and a snowy white starched and ironed tablecloth on top of the quilt. The prune box held the silver, plates, glasses and napkins — cloth napkins. If there were paper ones we country folk either didn't know about them or they were considered too expensive to use once and throw away. A quilt was spread on the ground on either side of the "table" for us to sit on. This was the only way we knew to have a picnic, on the ground under a tree.

A great deal of preparation went into the picnic fare. Our biggest stoneware mixing bowl was full of fried chicken, another held potato salad; there were deviled eggs, store-bought bread, cheese, crackers, pickles — both sweet and sour — a pan of macaroni and cheese, pork and beans straight from the can and a three-layer coconut cake. Rounding off this bounty was a large stone milk jar of lemonade made from fresh lemons and plenty of sugar. If the ice wagon was still around, either Grandpa or Uncle would walk across the bridge and buy a chunk to put into it, but if not, we drank it as it was and pronounced it delicious.

One of my most memorable Fourth of July picnics was the year of the Three Troubles, 1926, when we drove to the picnic in Grandpa's new Buick touring car. Grandpa's car created quite a stir with its shiny black body, the chrome glistening in the sun, its huge wooden-spoked wheels, the long hood covering its powerful motor. It was a splendid vehicle, standing in regal elegance among all the common cars. We were on display as we drove slowly in the procession toward the lake. People gawked at us as we drove along, the wind singing through the open sides, Grandma clutching her black taffeta bonnet, which she reserved for special occasions; me sitting on three folded quilts on the floor between the front and back seats; Auntie and Aunt Mattie in their shirtwaist dresses and Panama straw hats, Uncle and Grandpa wearing their Sunday pants and shirts. We had never before arrived anywhere in such style or with so much attention. Grandpa parked and immediately drew a crowd of curious spectators. It was his best day. He loved people and to talk and he had plenty of both all day. The only thing that could have improved the day was to have brought our picnic food in a trunk.

As farmers began looking anxiously toward the lowering sun, we knew the day's celebration was drawing to a close. Time to get moving so the chores could be done before sunset. Hot, dirty, sticky but with the complete satisfaction of a day well spent, we waved goodbye to each other. We had honored our country, our flag, our heroes and had a great time doing so. We left the celebration reassured that this was the best and greatest of all countries; confident it would remain so for the rest of our lives and for generations to come.

One of the first things a farmer did when putting up his farm buildings was dig a cellar. In West Texas this job was made easier than might have been because there were no rocks to work out of the ground or stop one's pick and shovel, and plenty of dry weather in which to work. The soil was rich brown as far down as a man wanted to dig. Most cellars measured about five feet deep, nine feet wide and eleven feet long. The walls and floor were left in their natural state — dirt. The raised roof was made of boards with dirt piled over it and a chimney-type vent extending from the ridge. When finished it resembled a small hill. Steps leading down into the cellar were dug and shaped and a wooden door laid above them at ground level, slanting toward the roof. The door was a neat place to roll one's ball up and down or slide down on one's bottom if no parent was watching. Kids were not allowed to play in the cellar nor run or walk on its roof.

Uncle built shelves on each side of ours to store canned fruit and vegetables, empty glass jars and the big preserving pans used in canning and jelly making. Onions, apples, potatoes and other staples were stored in baskets on the floor.

Besides being a perfect storage place both winter and summer, the cellar served as a haven of security and protection during severe storms which frequently came in summer. In fact, it was often spoken of as "the storm cellar." A shovel and hammer stood permanently in one corner for digging out in case some heavy object blew or fell onto the cellar door. A kerosene lantern hung on a nail from one of the rafters and a box of matches was kept on one of the shelves so we would have light while we were confined there.

Watching a storm build up is an awesome sight, your own uneasiness building with it. With a clear, uncluttered view, we could see the restless black clouds boiling up on the distant horizon long before it became a full-blown storm. Doggedly and persistently they inched their way up, rumbling from time to time as an ominous, surly, oppressive atmosphere stifled the air around us. The tempo picked up as the clouds steadily climbed higher and spread out, covering the sky; the constant rumbling thunder grew louder and louder as lightning streaked an erratic pattern in first one part of the clouds, then another, or struck a blow right down the middle, ripping the clouds apart. There followed a violent, deafening eruption, as if the sky was trying to belch up something indigestible. Soon the sun was cut off completely so that an eerie green darkness engulfed the land.

If Uncle was in the field plowing when a storm came up he would head quickly for the barn, get the mules unhooked, into the barnyard and unharnessed so they would not act as a ground for the lightning. A farmer out on a plow was a perfect target since the land was flat, the plows made of iron and farm buildings sparsely scattered.

It was at such times we "went to the cellar." The Hendersons, neighbors who lived less than half a mile up the road, did not have a cellar — probably the only farm in our community that did not have one. They frequently came to ours for shelter when it looked like a bad storm was coming. Often this was in late afternoon after a hot, sultry day. Maybe we'd be eating supper, Uncle getting up every few minutes to look out the back door to see how the clouds were building — whether it looked like rain or hail or a cyclone or just a lot of noise and wind. If he hurried back inside and said, "Get to the cellar!" no one fooled around. Auntie jumped up from the table and grabbed me by the hand; Uncle was already out the door; headed for the cellar. By the time we caught up with him he was straining against the wind to open the door. We'd hear voices and almost at once Hendersons were right behind us, Mr. Henderson helping with the door and following Auntie and me down the steps were Mrs. Henderson, her mother, Mrs. McCaslin and their son, E. J., who was my age and playmate. It was a big adventure to E. J. and me but serious and frightening to the adults. Seated on upturned boxes and buckets, the dusty, dank smell filling our noses and settling in our throats, we were prepared to wait out the worst of the storm. Safely inside, we listened to the roar of the wind and the deafening claps of thunder, the crackle and pop following a streak of lightning, hoping and praying it did not hit the house or barn. At times we heard the welcome sound of rain pouring down; sometime the dreaded sound of hail hitting the tin cover on the vent. Eventually, the rumble and roar faded and the howling wind died down. Apprehensively, Uncle and Mr. Henderson pushed up the door not knowing what they would see. It could be devastation, or water running in the ditches and filling all the low places — a welcome sight — or neither,only the cooled-off atmosphere after all the sound and fury, a big blowout.

Late in that memorable summer, 1926, such a storm blew up that it stays clearly in my mind. Uncle had an alfalfa patch cut and bales were lying in the field. After lunch on this particular day he hitched the mules to the wagon and headed for the field to pick up the bales and haul them to the barn. Auntie and I rode with him, Auntie to help, me for the adventure.

It was a hot, windless afternoon, the air dank and heavy. Our sweaty clothes stuck to our bodies, and the salty perspiration coursed in gritty lines down our faces, making our eyes water. The mules' flanks were white where the sweat had collected along their traces. We worked steadily, and it was middle of the afternoon when we first noticed the black clouds gathering across the length of the western horizon and steadily rising. We wanted to finish the haying so we ignored the growing nervousness of the mules, the occasional rumble of thunder and the darkening sky.

A sudden, violent gust of wind, knocking us off balance and wrestling a bundle of hay from Uncle's hands, followed by a suffocating stillness, finally got our undivided attention. Looking to the west we saw, moving in fast, an angry green-black cloud hanging low and heavy like a giant curtain ready to drop. Quickly, in near panic, we jumped onto the wagon and gave the mules their heads. They responded instantly, fright putting extra energy into their powerful muscles so they were half running with their heavy load. When we reached the barn, small as I was, fear gave me the strength to jump from the wagon and drag open the barnyard gate. Auntie, on the ground, clung doggedly to the mules' bridles; their nostrils flared and eyes wide with fright, while Uncle, steadying them with his commands, struggled to unhitch the trace chains from the wagon. This done, he skinned off the most burdensome part of their harness and freed them through the gate.

By now it was dark as night. The cloud seemed just above our heads, the lightning cutting across and lighting our way as we ran toward the cellar. Just as we reached the door we heard a shout over the roar of the wind and thunder and by a flash of lightning saw the Hendersons coming through the yard on a dead run. The men put their combined strength into holding open the door while the women and children clambered down the steps. The door was barely down and secured by the rope when the storm opened up. Our ears were molested by the constant, deafening clatter of hail on the vent cover and the roar of the wind as it drove the pellets into the ground. It went on and on; it seemed the noise would never stop, but it finally subsided into the mutterings of spent wind and clouds and an uneasy silence. When the men opened the cellar door we did not have to see the devastation to know it was there; we only had to look at their faces. Uncle and Mr. Henderson were as near tears as men of those times were permitted to be. But to me it was a blessed relief for, though I understood the enormity of this tragedy, I also recognized it as the last of my Three Troubles. If Granny Bailey was right, then at last I could breathe easy. While Auntie and Uncle, and many others in the county, tossed sleeplessly through the night, I was able to sleep peacefully and dreamlessly.

There would be no crops to harvest this fall. Destruction lay for miles in all directions. The storm cut a swath through the land, indiscriminate in its demolition, leaving futility and a bitter lump in the throats of work-weary farmers. All the endless days of toiling up and down the rows, sunup to sundown, the sweat, the tired muscles, the vigilant care — all for nothing. What an hour ago had been thriving, green healthy cotton stalks with squares beginning to produce tiny bolls, promising a bumper crop, now lay a hopeless, battered mass of stalks, leaves and squares beaten into the ground. The maize and corn and hegira, their proud, strong stalks broken and bent, lay in the rows as if slain by a ruthless army and left on the field to die. Carnage. At no time in a farmer's life does he feel such utter, complete defeat and despair — such agonizing helplessness and hopelessness as when he looks at a crop, almost ready to lay by, in total annihilation.

But they had resilience, these farmers. They had fought

the land itself to bring it into cultivation, they had survived those first years on faith and courage, they had overcome prairie fires, drouth, blizzards, had battled it all to get where they were now. They would square their shoulders and go forward. Courage would overcome despair and disappointment. Nothing could be gained by whining and wallowing in self-pity so the farmer got busy doing what he could — assessing the damage, clearing out the debris and salvaging whatever could be saved.

When a farmer lost his crop he lost his income. The cows, chickens and pigs became very important, for the cream, butter, eggs and sale of pigs were the only cash income until another crop could be grown and that was a year away. This called for careful planning. How long would the supply of feed in the barn and haystacks last the farm animals? How long would the canned beans, peaches, corn and other home-canned food sitting on the cellar shelves hold out to feed a hungry family? How could he save? Cut back? Next spring there would be the expense of buying seed to plant a crop. It went without saying that all luxuries and frivolities could be forgotten — there would be no new front room curtains, no new school dresses and no Christmas gifts.

So the farmer pulled up a chair to the kitchen table, opened his Big Chief tablet to a fresh page, took out his pocketknife and sharpened his lead pencil. Pulling the kerosene lamp a little closer, he set pencil to paper to do some intense figuring. In the wee hours of the night, alone, he came at last to determine his needs and he knew what he must do.

Next morning, swallowing his pride, he put on his Sunday pants and shoes, cranked up the Model-T and drove to town and the First National Bank, where he would sit down with Mr. Weakley and lay his problem before him. Bankers in rural West Texas understood and cooperated when disaster struck the farm communities. Frugal as most farmers were, it was not always possible to have put back enough cash money to see one through an entire year, plus the expense of putting in another crop. A good banker understood this. His business transacted, the farmer put this unpleasant task behind him, thanked the Lord it was not more than he could handle and proceeded to get on with the business of living.

Likewise, the farm wife and children readjusted their thinking and made their own compromises with the situation. It was a family farm and each member shared in whatever the season brought — a fine, prosperous crop, an ordinary one or one that was a complete loss. Whatever needed to be dealt with in farm life was approached with family solidarity — each one as important to the family unit as any other from the smallest child to the father, who was the undisputed head of the family. It was a safe, secure life — life on a farm in those dependable days of the '20s — a haven to house one's heart.

The cultivation of the crops and the main thrust of the growing season were over by the first part of August. It was time to watch and wait as the cotton and row crops matured into a bountiful harvest. All facets of farm life at this stage of the season were on the wane. The sun had moved slightly but noticeably southward. We were in the shank of summer.

AUGUST

August was a season unto itself. It was the lull between the busy days of summer, the beginning of harvest and then the new school year. Not to say an idle time — it was a busy month but in a different way.

The crops were laid by early in the month so there was little or no field work; however, Uncle walked over the field almost daily to see how the feed stuff was maturing and the cotton bolls growing, pulling a few careless weeds here and there that had evaded the go-devil blades or the hoe. What the garden produced now was for immediate consumption since preserving and canning had been done at the peak of the season. The mules were turned out to pasture to rest up for the harvest and the listing that would come after the harvest. The corn was taller than a man and the maize, kefir and other grain stood lush and green, their long leaves rustling in the August wind. The cotton stalks waved lazily in the hot sun, so important now to maturing of the bolls

Most farm work and chores could be finished by noon. The long afternoons provided Auntie time for the hand-work and sewing she loved to do. Uncle could move at a slower pace, and I could loll away the hours — delightful, delicious hours.

Some afternoons Auntie and I put on clean dresses and went visiting. Within walking distance were Mrs. Henderson, Mrs. Meador, Mrs. Morris, Mrs. Bullard and Mrs. Slusher. There was E.J., my age, at the Hendersons'; we had played together since we were toddlers and he'd as soon play dolls as war games or baseball. Lucile was at the Meador house. This was my favorite place to visit for Lucile and I played very compatibly together and she had the most enviable cache of toys!

She had every one she had ever received. They were put away in boxes and stored behind a faded green velour curtain which hung on a heavy wooden rod across a corner of the back bedroom. I never, to my great disappointment, was invited to go behind the curtain with her. She would disappear behind the curtain and in a space of time emerge with a box. After we had explored its contents and carefully replaced each toy in the box, she would disappear again, like a character in a Lewis Carroll book, and bring out another box. A beautiful doll with curly hair and blue glass eyes, dressed in a crinoline petticoat under a taffeta dress, still remained in her box. A narrow elastic band about her neck kept her from toppling out when she was held up to be admired. Lucile said she was too nice to be played with. She had a porcelain tea set, each dainty piece lying in its little cardboard compartment. Once I took out a cup to examine the little painted flowers on its side, dropped and broke it. Lucile cried and I panicked into stunned silence at the enormity of my crime; painfully embarrassed and full of remorse, I stammered out how sorry I was. The next time Auntie and I went to their house Lucile did not offer to get out her toys. This was a statement loud and clear that I was not to be trusted with her treasures, causing me acute discomfort, even though not a word was uttered.

At the Morrises' were two boys who, if they were not busy with chores, were glad to play with me. I played their games — cars, bat-the-ball, marbles, cowboys and Indians. When we went to the Morrises' I wore my khaki coveralls.

There was no one at Bullards' or Slushers' for me to play with, so when we visited these houses it was a tedious and tasteless afternoon spent sitting uncomfortably on a chair and listening to grown-up talk. As soon as it seemed polite to do so I would whisper in Auntie's ear, "Can I go outside?" "Yes," she would whisper back, "but stay in the front yard."

Since most of our family were farmers August was the one month in the year when they could get away from the farm for a few days to visit relatives who lived too far away for regular visits.

Grandpa, Grandma and Aunt Mattie took me with them to visit relatives in Shallowater and Littlefield. Today with our fast cars and wide paved roads, the drive would probably take less than three hours, but in the '20s, in

Grandpa's Buick, over gravel or dirt roads that followed the straight lines and sharp angles of the section lines, it was not a trip to take lightly. Only twice do I recall making the long trip to Gorman, about two hundred miles away, where Aunt Rosa, Uncle Bob and various distant relatives lived, and where my aunts and uncles had grown up. It was an all-day trip, leaving at first light and arriving about sundown.

During August we were constantly alert for the arrival of relatives. We never knew what day it would be; when a letter came in the mail from an aunt saying they would come, there was only a general reference to the date of arrival. It depended upon a number of eventualities — whether a neighbor or friend could be found to "look after the things" while they were away, whether there was still garden stuff to gather and put up, and whether the church revival would have been held. So we would wait and watch and be prepared. Just as surely as we let down our guard and planned a little trip of our own, or failed to clean the house or cook a big meal, a carload would pull up in our drive, cousins falling out of the car on the run and grown-ups calling out greetings, laughing and hugging. Sudden and welcome excitement! As soon as the suitcases were brought inside, the women went to the kitchen and started cooking supper; Uncle took the men to look at the crop, the young heifers, the pigs; the kids got into a rousing game of some sort.

In retrospect, since there were more boy cousins than girls, we seemed always to play "rousing games" or games that were suitable to both — hide-and-go-seek, blindman's bluff, I spy, Annie over, punch-the-icebox, pussy-wants-a-corner (on the roof of Grandpa's big brooder house where we were out of sight of grown-ups).

Sometimes we played "house" but with a definite masculine slant.

After supper, and after we had played through the long West Texas twilight, was the most fun time of all for us kids for we were allowed to continue our fun and games after it was dark. This uncommon activity turned the night into a special event. The drone of adult voices from the porch formed a secure background for hiding behind rose bushes and around corners of the house to jump out and scare each other, or for a game of punch-the-icebox, or to "put on a program" for our own enjoyment — one of us acting as the emcee to introduce the "performers" who sang songs, recited poems, told jokes or stories — all of them worn out from much use but heard with renewed interest in the glamourous nighttime setting. The star-filled sky hung low and bright, almost within reach if we stood on tiptoe. The moon, a huge lustrous globe, put out an intense, intoxicating light creating an aura of sweet strangeness. In this setting an enchantment took possession of us. We cavorted and danced and laughed and ran for the pure magic of it all.

Since all good households had two mattresses on every bed, there was no problem bedding everyone down. The extra mattresses were pulled from the beds and put on the floor in the front room. Made up with sheets, quilts and pillows they created comfortable, special sleeping arrangements for we children and an environment that prompted romping, turning somersaults and paroxysms of giggles. This exhilarating fun continued unabated until an aunt or uncle came into the room to settle us down. After the roughhousing stopped, we'd lie in the dark, moonlight sifting through the open windows, and tell the most gruesome ghost stories we could imagine. This would go on until the younger ones cried for us to stop, or we could, all at once, not hold our eyes open a minute longer.

Next morning the fun started all over again. Kinfolk from nearby came over for the day — more cousins, aunts and uncles to add to the pleasant confusion. The women spent most of the morning in the kitchen cooking large quantities of the best of good food. The men, after chores were done, sat in the yard under a shade tree and talked until the women sent them off to town to buy a block of ice for iced tea. We kids played and made trips through the kitchen asking aunts for snacks and, when the ice was being chipped for the tea, hunks of ice to chomp on. By the time our turn came to eat we were famished. There was plenty of food, including both pie and cake, huge glasses of iced tea with plenty of lemon and sugar and maybe a freezer of ice cream.

Interrupting our games in mid-afternoon, one of the aunts would call, "You kids come! We've cut a watermelon!" They didn't have to call us twice; we came on the run. Watermelons were at their best in August. Early that morning Uncle had gone to the garden and thumped around in the vines until he found the largest, ripest one. It was brought into the house and put under the bed in the back room to keep cool. When eating time came it was laid out on the wash bench under the mulberry tree and with the big butcher knife Uncle split it long-wise down the middle. If the cut opened up ahead of the knife we knew it was a good one. The two halves lay open, exposing rich red meat, rows of black seeds, and smelling heavenly. We kids waited impatiently for the first succulent bite. It was not sliced into serving pieces; we all — men, women and children — gathered around the melon each with fork or spoon with which we cut out hunks. After the grown-ups stopped eating we kids pounced on the remains like a bunch of vultures, eating every morsel. Then with our spoons we "scraped" it, scraping every visage of red down to the green rind, then drinking the juice. It was a sporting matter to see how many scrapings we could get. By the time the last drop was consumed we were so full we were miserable, our stomachs hard as a rubber ball.

By the end of the day, when we were called for supper, we were dirty, bedraggled and hungry. We'd line up at the kitchen sink to wash our hands and faces and comb our hair before we took seats at the table. After supper, remarkably revived, we were eager for an evening's adventure playing in the starlight. Alas, all too soon we were called inside to wash our feet and get ready for bed. To grown-ups it was unthinkable that we should go to bed without washing our feet. We kids looked upon it as a thinly disguised form of child abuse.

Washing one's feet before going to bed was a daily ritual in the summer when most children ran barefoot. "Did you wash your feet?" was a routine question put to all tired, sleepy farm kids before they fell into bed. It was a lot of trouble. The wash pan, which sat in the kitchen sink for the purpose of washing hands, face and feet, was filled halfway to the top with water, lifted down and set on the floor in front of a chair. The victim approached the chair as if he were marching to his electrocution, sat down, plunged one foot into the pan, soaped, washed and dried it. Then the other foot was subjected to the same persecution. When cousins were lined up waiting their turn to use the wash pan, this feeling of defiled sensitivity could spawn quarrels and harsh words — forgotten and forgiven, however, as soon as we fell upon our made-down beds and engaged in a good, hefty pillow fight.

Long, fun-filled days. When the morning came for them to leave it was a quite, subdued time — we were not ready for the visit to be over. When their car drove away and out of sight, a ribbon of loneliness wound around my heart and followed me into the empty, quiet house, lingering wherever I was for the rest of the day.

August was also the time when the neighborhood women and friends from around the community got together for all-day quilting parties. On these occasions the hostess had at least two quilts in frames, stretched and ready for quilting. Six to eight ladies could work comfortably around a quilt, so this meant there would be twelve to sixteen ladies and maybe a few onlookers who didn't quilt but who came to kibitz and enjoy the food and fun. They started gathering around nine o'clock in the morning, each one bringing a dish of food — salad, vegetable, pudding, pie, cake, fried chicken, sliced ham — good stuff — which was to be eaten at the noon break. There would be iced tea to go with the meal and strong, freshly percolated coffee to go with the pie and cake.

The quilters were eager to see what patterns the hostess had used to make her quilts. Wedding Ring, Dresden Plate, Nine Patch, Friendship, Log Cabin were favorites. The women used whatever was in their scrap box to piece their quilts — pieces left over from sewing dresses, aprons, blouses and other garments. Blending such a variety of colors and prints into a quilt that was pleasing to look at called for talent, artistry and an eye for design. There was not always a balance of light and dark or bold shades or pastels to work with, so the challenge was to see what one could make out of what one had. How attractively one could put it together made for friendly competition. It was a triumphant unveiling when a quilt was pieced, stretched onto the frames and displayed for the accolades of fellow quilters.

The ladies quilted from the time they arrived until far into the afternoon, fingers flying as they stitched and talked. A woman was known by the stitches she made for, like fingerprints, no two women made stitches the same. Some were small and even (greatly to be desired), some were small but uneven, some average, average but uneven, some too long but acceptable and some judged unacceptable on all points. If totally unacceptable, a quilter's stitches might be removed the next day and restitched by a more careful hand — in strict secrecy, of course. Mrs. Dalby was a case in point. She was everybody's favorite person; it would have been unthinkable not to invite her, for it was never as much fun when she was not present. She was lively, told funny stories, made witty remarks that kept the women laughing and was kind, helpful, a good friend to one and all. But her quilting, regrettably, fell into the totally unacceptable category. When she worked on a quilt of Auntie's or Aunt Mattie's it was removed and redone, but with a great deal of good humor. "Look at this, Mattie," Auntie would say as she ripped out stitches, "Can you believe anybody could make such a mess?" laughing as she said it.

It was a fun day with lots of laughter, good food, good fellowship and no small amount of gossip, when women who had so much in common could leisurely talk, share, and help each other. They went home in time to help with the evening chores, replete in a good and well-spent day.

Men took this time to visit back and forth between

farms. They could spend time sitting in the shade of a tree, perched on a barnyard fence or the back porch steps and have a friendly discussion during the lull of an afternoon.

The community churches furnished a special diversion during August, for it was then their revivals were held. They were scheduled to last a week but could last longer if enough collection was taken in at the services to make it worth the evangelist's time to prolong his stay. The revivals were given plenty of advance publicity through posters nailed to the telephone poles and fence posts along the county roads and on the front of Mr. Parrish's general store at Ragtown, our community center.

Farmers and their wives, with hard work behind them, were looking forward to some diversion. A week, or more if all went well, of nightly dressing up and stepping out was anticipated as happily as a round of social events. In fact, the revival served the purpose very nicely. A week of real social gatherings would have been frowned upon, whereas it was considered in the line of pious obedience to attend the revival meeting every night. This dedicated attitude was well accepted by the clergy since it would assure a good crowd at the services and generous donations in the collection plate — a satisfactory arrangement for both sides of the fence.

The evangelist and his song leader, who usually traveled with him, were expected to be housed at the parsonage of the host minister. The good pastor's wife would feed them breakfast but it fell upon the ladies of the congregation to provide the other two meals each day. So they were handed from one bountifully laden farm table to the next as each hostess tried to outdo the other in the quality and quantity she served.

There were two churches in Ragtown, the Baptist and the Church of Christ. There had been a Methodist church, of which my family were members, but the membership dwindled until it was eventually disbanded. The Baptist members did not attend the Church of Christ revival nor did the Church of Christ members attend the Baptist meeting, but the Methodists in the community, indiscriminately ecumenical, attended both, as did other denomination members who had no church home in the community.

The only noticeable difference between the two meetings was the setting. The Church of Christ held theirs outside under a tent, causing it to be labeled "tent meeting." Men of the congregation put up scaffolding and draped a tarpaulin over it to keep out the weather while the open sides allowed the breeze to circulate. The Baptists held theirs inside the church building and on a hot August night it could be uncomfortably warm even with all the doors and windows open. Cardboard fans, with the names of undertakers and funeral homes printed in bold black letters, lay on the benches for the comfort and convenience of the congregation. The rhythmic back and forth movement of the fans created a hypnotic effect, circumspect churchmen were caught nodding and tired children fell asleep. The Baptists, however, had a pianist and this addition lent a verve to the evening that was missing in the Church of Christ meeting since they did not allow musical instruments in their church services.

The evangelist was always well versed in the art of oratory. He preached long, scary, condemning, pleading sermons, designed to convince us that we were hopeless, lost sinners. He brought with him an energetic, charismatic song leader who, before the preaching began, led us in song. This was the part of the service we kids and young folk entered into with gusto. By the time the song service was over we were hoarse from our lusty singing of the familiar hymns — "Throw out the life line, throw out the life line, someone is sinking today," "When the roll is called up yonder, I'll be there," "On a hill far away stood an old rugged cross," and others, most of which we knew by heart. Then there was the special music, a duet, solo, or quartet made up of local folk, harmonizing their own arrangement of "In the Garden" or "Whispering Hope." Next, the offering plates were passed with an appeal from the local minister to give generously. After this bit of housekeeping was accomplished and the evening prayer was said by one of the church fathers, interspersed with an occasional "Amen" from fellow members in the congregation, we settled down, at last, for the sermon.

The evangelist began his sermon normally enough, actually bordering on the dull side, reading and elaborating on his text and building his foundation, word upon word. As his theme developed and he warmed to his subject, you could feel the gathering momentum. He carried his audience along much as a composer of music does in building up to a great crescendo, and at the end using every instrument in the orchestra. Likewise did our evangelist — pacing up and down in front of the lectern, waving his Bible, pausing for emphasis to let a choice morsel sink into our world-weary souls, then, letting the words roll out like summer thunder, he came at last to a dramatic close. Perspiration pouring from his brow, arms extended to gather us all into the bosom of the Lord, he gave the invitation to come down to the altar and "be saved."

While the congregation, under the able direction of the song leader, sang "Just as I am without one plea," he entreated sinners to come forward. Who will be first? Come. Come! When no one came down to take his hand and kneel at the altar, he stopped the singing and told us, in a quiet, emotion-filled voice, how sad it would be if we died and had not "been saved." As we resumed our singing he continued to give his impassioned plea. It was highly dramatic. And frightening and uncomfortably disturbing to my friends and me so that we, for once, sat grim faced and subdued, reflecting on our irreverent behavior and searching our jaded conscience for an unforgivable stain or blemish.

Of course, there would be some converts. Children of the church members were expected to "go down" if they had not previously joined the church. Someone, or maybe an entire family, who were from another denomination and wanting a church home, might "go down." Then there were those who we came to count upon; the few who went down to take the preacher's hand and tearfully confess their sins of commission and omission, who always did so — summer after summer, usually on the last night of the revival. Some irresistible force seemed to propel them down the sawdust trail.

My folk were not great on attending revivals; neither were Grandma and Aunt Mattie. Grandpa and I never missed one. He would drive by about sundown in his Buick, honk the horn and I'd go sailing out the front door. Sliding onto the leather seat beside him, I'd look up with a big grin and he'd look down at me, his bushy eyebrows shading his sharp black eyes, and grin back, giving me a big wink. We'd go happily off together, expectant, anticipating the evening ahead.

I sat with my girlfriends. The first one of us to arrive was expected to claim a bench far enough back to avoid monitoring from parents but not so far back we would miss anything. During the service we whispered, passed notes and giggled behind our songbooks. The boys had special benches they liked to occupy and carried on much as we girls did except they would surreptitiously nudge and elbow each other and make funny faces to distract us girls and each other. The young folk confiscated the back rows where, under the emotionally charged atmosphere of a summer night, romance waxed and waned. It was the perfect setting for flirtations, pairing off, hand holding and "speaking" looks into each other's eyes.

After the Amen was said and the main event was over, the social part began. Parents got in a good, much-needed visit. Women put out invitations to their quiltings, exchanged news and gossip; the men talked farm conditions and politics; the kids played, got into fights, told secrets; the young folk continued their romancing. Near the front of the tent a small knot of men would have gathered around the preacher where an animated theological discussion took place. Before long, it was obvious, to anyone taking notice, the discussion had heated up and sides were taken. Grandpa was the ring leader in this gathering for he dearly loved a good argument and was not particular which side he argued.

During the service Grandpa sat on one of the front benches, cocking his head so his left ear, where his hearing was sharpest, would be toward the preacher. He was not beyond abruptly inserting his own comments during the sermon. He did this from time to time, shocking the preacher into speechlessness, his words dangling in mid-air. A preacher might be quoting scripture to back up his statement, and Grandpa, totally absorbed in the sermon, would wave an arm at him and say, "Hold up, young man. Read the verse before your quotation so as to get the full meaning." This kind of thing is probably what gave my folks a distaste for revivals — the good chance they would have to endure the humiliation of just such behavior. It never embarrassed me; Grandpa was a student of the Bible and knew what he was talking about so I felt he was justified in correcting the preacher. How other folk in the congregation felt about it was never discussed in my presence nor, I suppose, in Grandpa's. He was a most respected man in the community so they probably rested their case on that premise.

Grandpa and I might not be the first to arrive at the meeting but we were always the last to leave.

The close of the revivals left a void in community activities. There was a letdown and restlessness for awhile. Most romances that had blossomed so hopefully, faded and died, while some came into full bloom becoming a lifetime commitment. Adults experienced a lack of enthusiasm as they resumed their normal routine. We kids were in the doldrums, missing the fun of our nightly meetings. However, this mood eventually dissipated as we became involved in the day-to-day pursuits of country living.

Going to town was always a special treat but going to town to buy fabric for new school dresses, and on a day not Saturday, was an event. On such a special day there was no thought of dallying around and wasting precious time. Before Auntie and Uncle had finished milking the cows and doing their other chores, I had washed and dried the breakfast dishes, made my bed and thrown grain to the chickens. Then, dressed in my voile dress and patent leather shoes, the elastic band under my chin hold-ing my black straw sailor hat firmly in place, and clutching the purse Aunt Mattie had given me for my birthday, I was ready to be on our way. The clock on the shelf above the dish cupboard slowly ticked off the minutes as I wait-ed in an agony of frustration for Auntie and Uncle to change into their town clothes.

We drove through our big front gate and across the culvert into the road, turned toward town. We reached the rim of the Caprock and started our descent. The road took us across the wide vista of rough lowland where Post lay, a few miles away, nestled snugly into the skyline. A lit-tle shiver of excitement danced down my spine as the town came into view. From my limited experience it seemed a metropolis of no small dimension.

There were three dry goods stores, all on the south side of Main Street: Stevens Dry Goods Store, Bryant Link and the store operated by the Jewish family. In the '20s almost all small West Texas towns had a Jewish family who owned and operated a dry goods store. They stocked a different line of merchandise than other stores, usually less expensive.

Uncle stopped the car in front of Bryant Link and Auntie and I stepped out onto the sidewalk. Like lifting the curtain on a stage to begin Act I of a play, we opened the heavy glass door and made our entrance. At once the tantalizing smell of "new" enveloped us — new shoes, new fabric, new hats, new dresses, a store full of new. Auntie walked purposefully toward the fabric department with me following close behind and, on reaching the counter, unfastened the clasp on her black leather purse and took out her list. At the kitchen table last night, in the light of the kerosene lamp, she had written, in her unique style, the list of fabrics, patterns, trimmings, buttons and all items necessary to make school dresses, skirts and other garments I would need to start a new season. Serious deliberation and planning had gone into this list and the fulfillment of it would be considered just as seriously.

Miss Vita, Auntie's favorite clerk, waited on us. She was a favorite of mine, too, for she gave me special attention; complimenting my big brown eyes and lifting me up to sit on the counter when I grew tired of standing. To demonstrate my infatuation for her, I once insisted on naming one of our newborn calves for her. When we were in the store some time after the christening, I excitedly made the announcement. If she was less than flattered for being so singled out, then I never knew for she graciously accepted my attempt to honor her.

The first order of business was a thorough study of the McCall's pattern book. McCall's was Auntie's favorite; no other patterns ever suited her as well. After long and serious consideration of every pattern in the girl's section she, with Miss Vita's help, made her selections and then turned her attention to the the colorful bolts of fabric stacked on the long shelves behind the counter. Miss Vita was kept busy reaching down bolt after bolt to be laid out on the counter so Auntie could make a close inspection. She must feel the quality and weight, try buttons, braid and rickrack against the various prints, plaids, solids and checks. I was an interested observer, the character with the non-speaking role, merely filling up space on the stage. But it was fun to watch as Auntie and Miss Vita coordinated and considered and talked over the desirability of one combination over another. If a color was in question, Miss Vita would roll a length of the fabric from the bolt and drape it around my neck to see if it was "becoming" to me. I could be sure that red would figure prominently in the choices, as would burnt-orange, navy blue, tan background with red, green or blue figures and flowers. And black checked gingham. Looking back, it seems I always had a black checked gingham dress in my wardrobe. Very small checks and trimmed with red bias tape. The closest color to the pink I longed for was a deep, soft rose or maroon.

At last selections were made. Miss Vita measured off the yards from the bolts, folded and stacked each piece on the counter beside the cash register. With the fabric there were patterns, bias tape, lace, braid, buttons, thread, elastic for the bloomers to be made to match the dresses, hooks and eyes, clasps, belt buckles and any special ornament that might "set off" the garment.

Miss Vita, ticket pad on a ribbon around her neck, pencil behind her ear, would look over our purchases. "Do you think of anything else, Mrs. Mangum?" Auntie, holding her hand to her chin, thoughtfully considering the stack of material she had selected, then systematically auditing it against her list, and at last, satisfied all was well, would reply, "No, I believe this is all." Miss Vita painstakingly recorded each item, in her bold, legible hand, on her ticket pad, added up the column of figures — twice, to make certain she had the correct total — then moved to the cash register and positioned herself to ring up the sale.

Cash registers of that era were intimidating in their austerity and magnitude. The one at Bryant Link was made of heavily embossed metal, the keys large and exacting in their importance as they announced a sale of merchandise with a loud clang that ended in a ring. It was a serious procedure, ringing up a sale, and an awesome experience to watch — if you were a little country girl who had never traveled further than the adjoining counties, and only then to visit kinfolk. At the same instant the bell rang, the cash drawer shot out so the clerk could deposit the money. When she pushed the drawer back into the bowels of the register another loud ring announced the end of the transaction.

Again Auntie unfastened the clasp on her black leather purse and reaching down into the bottom, brought out the bag that held the carefully saved butter and egg money. From this precious hoard she counted out the amount and gave it to Miss Vita. Miss Vita punched the appropriate keys for the total amount, pulled down the lever on the side of the register and as soon as she released it the clanging and ringing began and the drawer shot out. The butter and egg money disappeared as she closed the drawer and the final benedictory ring sealed the bargain.

A metal rack holding a huge roll of wrapping paper was attached to the edge of the counter near the cash register. It was usually brown, though some stores used white and some even had their name printed on it. Miss Vita expertly estimated the size sheet she needed, deftly tore it from the roll and wrapped the purchases, folding over the ends to make a neat package. Then from a tall cone of cotton twine which stood beside it she unwound what she needed to tie the package securely. It was essential that a clerk knew how to make a good neat package.

Our arms were full as we left the store and walked to the car where Uncle had been patiently waiting to drive us home. As soon as we were there we dumped all the packages on the kitchen table and begun untying and unwrapping so we could admire the beautiful things we had bought. There were lengths of lovely print fabric — enough for several school dresses, dark blue, red or soft rose velveteen for a Sunday dress and lace and buttons to trim it. Bright wool plaid for a skirt. There was black sateen for bloomers, soft white muslin for underskirts, cotton flannel for night gowns. Spilling out of a separate package were the patterns, trimmings and spools of thread. After we had looked and admired to our hearts' content, Auntie very carefully folded all the wrapping paper and wound the twine around the ball we were collecting. Good wrapping paper had many uses as did a ball of twine.

Next morning, as soon as chores were done, the kitchen table was cleared to be used as a cutting board. Auntie was soon absorbed in an activity she loved and was an expert in doing — sewing. She knew the special touches that made a garment smart and stylish.

After the dresses were made they were hung in the big walk-in closet in the back bedroom in readiness for the new school year. Hardly a day passed by that I did not go into the closet to look at and fondle each and every garment, making and changing a dozen times my decision about which dress to wear that all-important day — the first day of school.

A subtle change came over us as the last days of August loomed on the calendar. Sobering thoughts tinged with excitement. The long, busy and often lazy days of summer were fading away, slipping from our grasp. The roses were a sorry lot, their petals shattered on the ground; the few remaining melons and cucumbers, clinging to the dried-up vines, would be the last; the roosters had grown too big for frying, some were trying to crow — experimentally, in hesitant, teenage voices; green apples were hanging heavy on the trees. These changes turned our minds toward the days that lay ahead. School would soon open; harvest would begin. The air smelled different, and the wind had taken a turn. Summer was over.

FALL

It was like a heavy line had been drawn after August thirty-first, marking the end of summer and the beginning of fall, with the first day of school highlighted in bold red numerals. To us Ragtown schoolchildren, the opening day of school was more like New Year's Day than the day itself.

That first day was a big celebration — kids spilled onto the school ground from all directions, walking, riding horseback, some, like myself, brought in the family car. Painfully obvious in our new school clothes, we girls in our homemade dresses and the boys in new overalls and shirts and all of us hoping we could get through that first

day without scuffing up our new shoes. Our school supplies — a new unsharpened pencil, pencil box, Crayolas
and a Big Chief tablet, the pupil's name written prominently on the red cover just above the picture of the
Indian chief — were caught over our shoulders in new
book satchels. Satchels tended to be made from the
same pattern, whether store-bought or homemade.
They were square and wide enough to accommodate a
geography book or drawing book and deep enough to
carry all our other books and supplies. A flap at the top
folded over and buttoned or fastened with a snap, a slim
pocket on one side held a pencil box and some had an
outside pocket to hold one's lunch. They were made of
a heavy coated fabric if store-bought and otherwise
made of mattress ticking or ducking. Satchels were for
carrying books back and forth between home and
school. We took them home every night (or were supposed to do so) to "bring up our lessons" or "get our
lessons." "Homework" was not part of our vocabulary
in those days.

Whether it was the keen excitement with which some of
us met that first day or the reluctant steps of those who
hated to study and dreaded the confinement of the
schoolroom, the smell of freshly oiled floors mingled with
the aroma of new Crayolas, new shoes, books, and the
faint, lingering musty, dusty smell of a classroom that had
been closed since mid-May, worked like hypnotic incense
to lure us back into the cloistered walls.

Animated, talking too loud, shouting to friends, we
hugged our best girlfriends and walked arm-in-arm, sometimes four abreast, across the schoolyard. Boys poked
each other, teased, shoved and hooted at each other, all
with the same meaning as the arm-in-arm of the girls.

Happily anticipating sharing another long school year — playing together, competing against each other, learning together, sharing confidences and whispered bits of gossip, staying overnight at each other's houses — it was not only a reunion with friends but with all classmates. We were glad to see the troublemakers, the ones we poked fun at and the quiet, shy ones. We were all bound together in a great comradeship. We were ready for the adventure of another school year together and whatever it had to offer.

Our teacher was at the door to greet us and the rows of empty desks stood ready, inviting us to claim them. There was a scramble for choice seats — most kids wanted to sit beside their best friend and as far away from the teacher's desk as possible and, on this first day, no issue was made of it. The boys made a beeline for the back seats, the McNabb twins and I challenged one and all for the front ones, and everyone else fell in between. As could be expected, by the second week of school the teacher had sized up her students. She knew which pair needed to be separated, who could be trusted at the back of the room and the best location for the troublemakers so that she could keep them under surveillance. Amid much confusion and no small amount of grumbling, we moved into our newly assigned seats. We came to accept this change as inevitable yet hoping fervently that we did not end up sitting the whole year beside a pesky boy who hid our pencil and Crayolas or by someone who did not bathe often enough or who copied from our paper during examinations. Nevertheless, we did not argue with the teacher's assignment; her word was law in the classroom. We took our new seats with as much grace as we could muster and learned to live with whatever misfortune the change brought. There were twelve to fifteen students in a class with two classes occupying a room. First and second grades together, third and fourth, fifth and sixth. These three rooms were on the first floor along with a fourth which served as the library and Mr. Robinson's office, where he taught the upper-grade math classes. Seventh, eighth, ninth and tenth grades were on the second floor in two classrooms. The rest of the second floor was an auditorium.

That first day was a short one, letting out soon after lunch. It was a busy day. After the teacher had written our names down in her record book, appraised us of the rules of the classroom, the playground rules and school rules in general, books were passed out. We always hoped for new books; they smelled so good and there was a feeling of importance attached to a new book and knowing you were the first to handle it, to open it and study it. More often than not they were used. The state of Texas provided our books, and it was impressed upon us that they were only loaned to us for the school year and we were to treat them with respect. Do not write in the margin. Do not turn down the corner of a page. Do not highlight by underlining sentences or paragraphs. After the books were passed out, we were given book covers and a period was given over to placing the covers on our books. Covers were made of heavy brown paper especially designed to fit each book. There were instructions where to cut and where to paste and the results should have been neatly covered books. Unhappily, this was not always the case. My own, for example. Invariably, I cut too deep or not deep enough and got my corners wrinkled. Long before the end of the school year the covers would be worn or torn and abandoned but, at least, we would start the school year in conformity with government rules and regulations.

At some time during the day we lined up at the pencil sharpener which was mounted on the wall at the end of the blackboard and waited our turn to put a sharp point on our new pencils. All summer we had sharpened pencils, when the occasion arose, with a pocketknife or a kitchen knife but to thus desecrate our school pencil was beyond thinking when there was a splendid sharpener in each classroom. I, for one, was so fascinated with it I could sharpen away a whole pencil in one day. This was the reason I was supplied from home with cedar pencils which cost a penny each instead of a brightly colored one which cost a nickel.

The whole object of school was to learn, to educate. We studied reading, spelling, arithmetic, writing, art, and by third grade we had language books and at some point history and geography. It is amazing how the teacher could teach two classes of all these subjects, instill in her students the importance of each lesson and individually instruct, when necessary. While Miss Riley, who for years taught third and fourth grades, was teaching third-grade reading, the fourth grade had been set to do arithmetic problems. While she taught the fourth grade arithmetic, the third grade was doing their art assignment. While she went over the art assignment with third grade, the fourth worked on writing skills. And thus she coordinated her day. This was the system other teachers in the Ragtown school and in other community schools used to teach. There were no free periods nor teachers' lounge. Teachers took breaks at recess when the children did, on the school ground.

In addition to regular classroom work, the teacher spent whatever hours were necessary in planning and helping in the production of any school activity her classes were involved with, such as programs, plays, class parties and other similar events. All teachers were expected to attend church every Sunday and to participate in church activities however they were requested to serve. Lady teachers were required to live in the teacherage — as the house was called — on the school ground especially for their use. Next door stood another house where the superintendent and his family lived. Men teachers got room and board across the road from the school at the Martin house.

There was always a man employed for the upper grades. He taught science, government and agriculture and coached the boys' basketball team. Coaching the basketball team was incidental to teaching — no one was ever hired for the purpose of coaching a team. That was a position unheard of in a country school in the '20s. Nevertheless, he was expected to fill this position. The team practiced during the recess periods; boys had farm work to do after school in the afternoon. In the spring he coached the baseball team and the field events. Mr. Robinson coached the girls' basketball team. Since he was a married man with a family this was acceptable. Lower-grade teachers were paid sixty dollars a month and upper-grade teachers slightly more for the eight-month term.

Assignments were made for the next day's lessons and we were expected to take our books home and study them. I cannot speak for the other students, but this was my first priority when I got home. I was given time to have a good snack and to tell Auntie all that had happened at school that day but after this brief reprieve I "got my lessons" for the next day. This was not my idea; I'd rather have gone outdoors to play but it was Auntie's and it stuck. At night after supper I was quizzed on all my assignments. My papers were gone over and if there were mistakes I worked until I got them right. I have reasons to believe not all parents were as strict about homework.

A large iron bell, mounted at the top of a wooden tower and rung by pulling a bell-rope, stood at the north entrance of the school building. Its ringing summoned us to class in the morning and from the playground at the end of recess. It rang twice in the morning — at eight-thirty to warn us, and again ten minutes later. After that we were tardy. Arriving late to your classroom was not to be taken lightly; it was a serious misdemeanor and your times tardy were recorded at the end of the month on your report card. What is more, it required some explaining, on the spot, to your teacher. "Last bell" carried a ring of authority that we respected.

When the bell rang we lined up to go inside — two rows at the south entrance and two rows at the north entrance, marching into the wide hall that ran the length of the building and into our rooms.

Recesses were as important to us and as much a part of our learning experience as the hours we spent in class. There were three — one at mid-morning, an hour-long one at noon, and another short recess in the afternoon. These times were unstructured; the only restrictions being we were not permitted to leave the school grounds nor go inside the building. We could enter into games with our classmates, go to a secluded spot with our best friends to talk or play some special game, or sit alone and do nothing — it was our time to use as we wanted to use it. Teachers were around to intervene if two boys got into a fight or if a child was hurt, but otherwise we were unsupervised.

The boys played baseball, marbles, mumble-peg, shinney and rough-and-tumble games suitable to boys. We girls had our own games, red rover, break the walls of China, drop the handkerchief, in and out the windows, crack the whip, mulberry bush, London bridge, statue. These were marvelous games and any number could play. Sometimes the boys joined us for a game of red rover, crack the whip or break the walls of China.

In most games we chose sides. There was no one to tell us we had to include a certain child or we had to make concessions for any of the weak or inept players. This minority group was always included but it was at the end of the side-choosing. They knew they would be chosen and without any outside pressure from teachers. This truth did a lot for their ego and their appreciation of the fairness of the system. Being last to be chosen carried no stigma; it was a fact they lived with and accepted.

At school and at home we organized and managed our own games without adult intervention. In this way we learned to get along with each other. We learned team play, how to take turns. We learned to be the one in charge and how to step down gracefully when our turn was over. We learned to play by the rules; to always play our best or suffer the hoots of derision from our playmates. We felt keenly the censorship among our peers when we cheated, or lied, or got mad because we lost the game. We learned to play fair, how to "take it" and how to be a good sport. It was excellent preparation for life in the Big World.

The noon recess buzzer was the most welcome of all because our stomachs had been growling through most of the last period. We were ready for our lunch. Lunches were brought from home in a variety of containers. It might be a store-bought lunch pail, bright red with flowers or figures painted on it, or it could be an empty lard bucket, or lunch might be wrapped in newspaper or held in a brown paper sack. The containers were as varied as the households from which they came, as were the lunches themselves.

Lunch might be a sandwich made from store-bought bologna or from bacon or sausage, left from breakfast, stashed inside a biscuit or something left over from supper the night before. It might be crackers and cheese or a cold baked sweet potato. Peanut butter was a favorite. It came in a little brown striped tin bucket. The oil accumulated at the top of the bucket and had to be stirred into the butter for there were no additives to keep it a creamy consistency. It was pure peanuts — nothing more. It was good mixed with chopped-up raisins and spread on slices of home-cooked bread. Most every lunch had an apple or a pear which came from the home orchard and either cookies, a big slice of layer cake or a fried fruit pie. The fried pie was made that morning while breakfast was being prepared. Not fancy lunches but good wholesome food to fill the stomach of a growing boy or girl.

We ate our lunch wherever we found a convenient place — on the schoolhouse steps, sitting against the building out of the wind, on the ground under one of the elm trees that stood on each side of the front entrance to the school grounds. On very cold days or when there was a bad sandstorm we were permitted to eat at our desks. In an orderly, neat fashion, of course. There was no throwing food nor boisterous action; that was saved for out of doors and there was punishment for those who might forget this rule.

To end the long noon recess, there was a first bell

which served as a warning to bring your game to an end; or if you and your best friend were sitting in some far-off, secluded part of the grounds, like on the east side of the Baptist Church which sat on the southeast corner of the school ground, where you had spent the time telling secrets and daydreams, you knew it was time to stand up, dust off the back of your skirt and get moving. Its main purpose was to remind one and all that they had fifteen minutes to make a trip to the toilet before marching back into the classroom. The girls' toilet was a "four-holer" behind the school building, backed up to the north boundary of the school ground. The boys' was located across the width of the grounds in the northeast corner and a considerable distance from the girls'. This was to insure that no hanky-panky took place.

However, this careful planning was challenged one day when Cleddie, out of burning curiosity and more boldness than wisdom, decided to go into the girls' toilet, just to see what it was like, as he later explained to Mr. Robinson. He chose the very end of recess to make his investigation, when it should have been safe to dash quickly inside, take a look and dash out. But it was his misfortune that Jewel and some of her friends were still inside. Not doing anything, we finally learned — just killing time until they had to go line up. But the surprise at seeing a boy in the girls' toilet shocked Jewel into action. She left the scene on a dead run to report to her teacher this shocking intrusion upon a female stronghold and as she ran she announced, in the manner of Paul Revere and his historic ride, "Cleddie came in the Girls'!" Before many minutes had passed the whole school knew about Cleddie's escapade. It is logical to assume he was in some way punished, though we never heard what nor how. For the next few days all the boys went around grinning in a snickering sort of way and all the girls were touchy and on the defense.

School let out at four o'clock. It had been a long day and both students and teachers were glad to hear the last bell of the day ring. Last periods were tedious; last period restlessness has been an affliction that has infested the schoolroom for as long as there have been institutions of learning. It's difficult to sit still and listen to that last lesson and to recite answers with any enthusiasm when the body is tired, the mind depleted and the stomach longing for a big slice of cake. Things happened during those last minutes that would not have happened at any other time of the day. Whispered quarrels that would burst into a full-fledged fight on the road home. A sudden onset of the giggles over nothing or the overwhelming urge to throw a spitball at the teacher's back while she wrote assignments on the blackboard, bang an arithmetic book over the head of the kid at the desk in front of you or give a smart-aleck answer to a teacher's question. This happened once when we were having an arithmetic test in the last period. Mr. Robinson saw Chilly Mason staring at the questions on the blackboard and making no attempt to write down the answers. "Are the questions hard?" Mr. Robinson asked him and Chilly answered, "Oh, no, but the answers sure are." We don't know where Chilly ran across that old, even then worn-out joke nor how he had the wit, if not the wisdom, to recall it at an apropos moment. We kids laughed. Mr. Robinson did not think it was funny. Chilly went home with his tail between his legs. Teachers are short on patience and have no sense of humor last period.

There was a great noisy exodus when the last bell finally

rang. Ragtown sat on a crossroads where two graded county roads met so after school was dismissed kids spilled out in all directions.

There were rules covering behavior on the roads to and from school. There was to be no fighting or abuse of anyone. Once a student was home he was out of the school's jurisdiction but until he turned into his own gate he was under the authority of school rules. There was nothing said about horse racing or foot races or stopping to play games but intimidation or abuse of another student was not tolerated. In spite of the dire threats and promises of inevitable punishment when found out, from time to time the rules were broken. One of my most frightening experiences, during my early school days, was seeing two older boys on horseback gallop up, fall off their horses and start beating up on one of the boys who walked in our group. The others, alarmed at the unexpected attack and concerned about the consequences, nevertheless stopped to watch the fight and to urge the victim to fight back. Some of we younger ones were upset by the victim's bloody nose and frightened at the anger and violence. I began to cry and one of the older girls pulled me close against her and walked me away. I still remember the comforting safety I felt with her strong arm around me and how she gently turned me around so I could not see the awful scene.

Every Thursday morning before noon recess, the student body attended chapel in the big auditorium on the second floor. Long rows of attached seats, laid out in a fan shape with a center aisle, faced the stage that stood across the southeast corner of the room. Each grade had an assigned section. The first and second grades on the front rows, graduating back to the upper grades at the rear.

Chapel was opened with a prayer followed by singing

the national anthem. Mr. Robinson made any announcements pertinent to school activities and then we sang several songs from the *Golden Book of Songs.* "Old Kentucky Home," "Carry Me Back to Old Virginny," "Dixie," "Onward Christian Soldiers," "Flow Gently Sweet Afton," "Row, Row, Row Your Boat" (which we sang as a round) and many more of those old songs. We loved to sing; the auditorium rang with our young voices.

After the singing we had a program. Sometimes the Mason family played for us. Lillie Belle played the piano, one of the boys played the mandolin, one the banjo and one the guitar. We liked to hear them play their music; they were students, like us, and we were proud of them. Once my city cousin heard them play and made fun of them. I angrily put her in her place by telling her she wouldn't know good music if it bit her and their music pleased us just fine! Most usually the classes took turns giving the program. Special entertainers were brought in from time to time. Once a professional storyteller came and held us transfixed with his dramatic renditions. I remember, before I was old enough to go to school, reciting "The Wonderful World" from the stage. On that same day Mozelle Manley's little brother recited a funny poem about when the preacher came to call. Occasionally, one of the local ministers spoke to us. On the whole we enjoyed chapel; it was a good experience.

School days in the '20s were good days. The discipline, routine and authority were not considered a hardship; rather, we found these strictures to be a good compass to steer us through those uncharted seas of learning.

Mr. Parrish's store, an old-fashioned general store, was an important part of our community and an integral part of our school days. We kids liked to hang around the candy counter, drooling over the display of candy bars — O'Henry, Baby Ruth, Bit O'Honey, Hershey Bars and Peanut Patties. There was a box of chewing gum on the candy counter and a glass jar that held what was then all the rage, OBoy, an oversized stick of gum in a yellow wrapper with OBOY printed in blue letters down the length of it. It made quite a mouthful. When all the sweet was chewed out it could be stretched the length of one's arm or could form a triangle if the edge of the wad was grasped between thumb and forefinger of both hands and pulled out and apart. And it could be popped louder than any other kind. It had numerous possibilities. Many contests grew out of these wads of gum. It had to be cut from one's hair if one got too show-offish and to remove it from clothing was next to impossible. It was not our parents' favorite treat for us. It cost a penny a stick, whereas the traditional packages, Wrigley's, Juicy Fruit and Spearmint, cost a nickel and could not perform all the interesting feats of OBoy.

From time to time Mr. Parrish would have special things that tickled our fancy. Once he had taffy candy, soft and in the shape of a donut which had a playing marble in the center. One year, before Easter, he brought in chocolate bunnies the size of a real bunny. I was not allowed to buy one but I watched with envy as my classmates came across the road from the store carrying these delectable-looking works of art.

Lucile Meador bought one. We were in the same classroom; I was third grade and she fourth, so that her seat was on the west side of the room and next to a window. On this particular spring day the weather was unseasonably warm. Lucile bought her rabbit when she arrived at school that morning but instead of eating it at recess, like the other kids did, she set hers on the window sill by her desk where the wind blowing through the open window would keep it cool enough so, hopefully, it would not melt. She carried it outside with her during recesses and continued to coddle it, standing under the shade of one of the two elm trees on the school ground. She talked to it, much to the amusement of fellow class members, saying, "Please little bunny don't melt; I want to show you to mother and daddy." Behind her back we made signs of throwing up. She kept her vigil all day, and surprisingly, it did not melt to any great extent, so she did get home with it to show to mother and daddy. I know because Mr. Meador and Uncle took turns driving us to and from school and it was Uncle's turn. Lucile nursed the bunny tenderly all the way home, continuing her encouragement into its chocolate ears. Did I have things to tell at school the next day!

Mr. Parrish had all the necessary school supplies in his store. Nickel pencils and cedar pencils for a penny. Tablets were a nickel and Crayolas fifteen cents. He had jars of paste, erasers, pens and ink and notebook paper with ring binders for the upper grades. If we needed any of these items we had better remember to purchase them before we entered the school grounds for once we were inside those encircling boundaries we had to get permission to leave from Mr. Robinson. And none of us were eager to encounter Mr. Robinson — though he was an understanding person — for any reason other than dire emergency.

In cold weather, after our home-orchard fruit had played out, there would be a bushel basket of red apples sitting on the floor of Mr. Parrish's store and maybe oranges, too. Always there was a stalk of bananas hanging by a rope from the ceiling. When one asked to buy a banana Mr. Parrish took a sharp, vicious-looking knife and cut it off the stalk. Fruit was sold by the piece (usually it cost a nickel) or by the dozen or half dozen. He kept a scant supply of foodstuff that a farm woman might need in an emergency, but he always had bakery bread and crackers and boxes of assorted cookies. There were small boxes of lemon cookies, gingersnaps and vanilla wafers which could be had for ten cents a box. The box held a dozen cookies.

There was a Magnolia Gasoline Company pump in front of his store, an air hose, a barrel with water in it and a bucket with a pouring spout so if the radiator of your car needed water it was there for you to use. Gasoline was twelve cents a gallon. When you pulled up to the pump Mr. Parrish asked how many gallons. You gave your order, "five gallons." He grasped hold of the long pump handle mounted on the side and pumped up five gallons into the tall glass receptacle above the pump; then, taking the hose from its hook, he emptied the gas into the tank of your car. He had oil, inner tubes and tires, generally called casings. And at the back of the store he kept certain hardware items a farmer might need until he could get to the bigger stores in town.

A coal stove sat in the middle of the store and Mr. Parrish had the wisdom to leave it standing the year round — none of the hassle of taking it down in summer and having to set it back up in the fall like farm homes did. I expect men like my grandpa and Uncle Steve Williams spent many comfortable winter afternoons seated in cane-bottomed chairs pulled up to its warmth, swapping stories and arguing politics and religion. The store was a sociable and pleasant place. Mr. Parrish was always kind and patient with the school children. We often called him Uncle Tom Parrish, just as many people called my grandpa Uncle Tom Vaught and Mr. Williams Uncle Steve Williams. It was a title of respect and affection commonly used in the '20s.

County fairs have not changed much down through the years. To describe one is to describe them all. The Garza County Fair was held after school started but before cotton picking began. The stock and animal exhibits and the crafts and food entries were as hotly contested as they are today. To enter a stall or booth and find a ribbon hanging on your entry, whether it was a prize bull or a lace doily, was just as exciting, but not more so, than it is today.

We farm kids were interested in seeing if anyone from our community won a ribbon. We walked through all the exhibits to see the fine animals and poultry: the big cage where Slusher's peafowls preened themselves and spread their tail feathers, the white rabbits, the goats, the banty roosters and other species we seldom saw. Also, the artistically decorated cakes and the delectable-looking pies, carrots and beans and beets arranged artfully in glass jars, and the multitude of handwork from quilts to tatting, dresses to bonnets. This walking and looking was done first to get it out of the way so we could put our full attention on the things that really counted — the rides.

We kids were particularly interested in the Ferris wheel and the merry-go-round. Most of the time it was the little kids who rode the merry-go-round while the big kids rode the Ferris wheel. Only once did I purchase a ticket to ride the Ferris wheel. Lucile Meador and I were together. She was more adventurous than I was. She said, "Let's ride the Ferris wheel; I've always wanted to." I said, "No, it's too high and when they stop it the seats at the top swing back and forth." I was scared just looking up at it. It seemed to tower higher and higher the more I looked at it. "Oh, come on, girl! Please ride it with me!" Not wanting to be a poor friend and always easily talked into things I didn't really want to do, I said I would. Reluctantly I reached into the pocket of my dress and pulled out my handkerchief. In one corner was tied my dime that I had been saving to have one last ride on the merry-go-round. I untied it and placed it in the dirty outstretched hand of the Ferris wheel operator. When the wheel stopped for us I had to force my reluctant feet to mount the loading platform and take a seat beside Lucile. The operator shut out my last possible hope of escape when he drew the bar across our seat and fastened it with a snap.

Before I had time to think, we were ascending into space, leaving my stomach back on the ground where we had been standing. Then the wheel stopped to let on passengers and Lucile and I were at the very top of it, swinging merrily. Lucile was grinning and enjoying the thrill of the sky above and the good earth miles below. I was screaming my head off. "Let me off! Let me off!" could be heard over a good part of the fairgrounds, along with my bloodcurdling screams. When we finally began our descent and reached bottom the operator was more than glad to get rid of me. I believe Lucile stayed on and finished her ride — alone.

We were fascinated with the sideshows — the fat woman and the dwarf, the strong man with his bulging muscles, the fire eater, the knife eater and the exotic dancer. There were the booths where we tried our skill at knocking over all the dolls lined up at the back of the booth and got a prize if we did, hit the big scales with a hammer to see how high the gauge went, and the shooting gallery where the boys congregated. There were the strange-looking barkers who chanted about their wares, tempting us to try everything, as they called to us to "Win a Kewpie Doll," "Only ten cents to see the Great Contortionist! See him twist his body in unbelievable knots!" These were the attractions that had us talking and planning about the fair for days before it opened, and we remembered them long after the prize ribbons were faded and forgotten.

It is doubtful the county fair ran more than three days. Country kids and their families went on Saturday. All the county farmers turned out to see their own and others' entries, socialize and take a much-needed break in their routine workdays.

Autumn in West Texas has never been known for its color. Elm, locust, mulberry and orchard trees do not flame with brilliant colors; rather, the leaves wilt, dry up and blow off so that one day the limbs are bare with only a few brave leaves clinging tenaciously in the prevailing wind. The cottonwoods around the draws below the Caprock and around Yellow House Canyon turned yellow, but the wind usually had blown most of the leaves away before we had a chance to see them. This does not mean, however, that we did not have our own special autumn colors. We had the brilliant blue of the October sky, spectacular sunsets and breath-taking nights of golden moon glow. Added to this palette were the bright yellow splashes of ripened pumpkins lying in the faded gardens and rich gold of harvested fodder standing in shocks over the fields.

And there was the great harvest moon. Slowly it made its way over the edge of the eastern horizon into the last rays of the fading sunset. Majestically, it rose into the sky, spreading its golden glow over the vast flat plains, transforming the landscape and everything it touched with its magic. The windmill became a silent, silver giant and the vulnerable orchard trees looked like rows of ghosts against the mellow glow. A hush fell over the farm animals — even the neighborhood dogs were quiet. It was a time of enchantment, otherworldly, stirring the imagination, filling one with awe, the beauty and majesty almost beyond bearing, our special autumn treat.

Sunsets in West Texas at any season of the year are spectacular. But in the autumn they are at their best. By the time the sun is a hand-high from sundown it is a fiery red ball, dropping slowly, coloring the sky the length and breadth of the horizon. A panorama of red-orange, rosy-pink, pink, lavender, purple and mixtures of these we had no name for, splashed across the western sky as if some celestial artist had swished his mammoth brush and created his masterpiece. Gradually, the brilliance softened, changing to pastels, fading until only a faint dusty-rose ribbon hugged the rim between earth and sky. Then the long twilight set in, suspended between the dark of night and the light of day, a quiet light hanging like a curtain of gauze over fields and farms, slowly disappearing into darkness. An autumn sunset on the plains of West Texas is like a holy benediction.

Added to the colors of autumn were its smells. The row of apple trees in our orchard hung full of fruit ready to be picked. The overripe ones that had fallen on the ground and were beginning to rot had a rich, winey smell. These apples were not big shiny ones like Mr. Childress sold in his store but were scrawny little things — sweet, crunchy and satisfying. From the kitchen came the mouth-watering aroma of baking sweet potatoes. The whole outdoors was permeated with the heady smell of hay being cut and bundled. It lingered on long after it had been stacked into wigwam-like shocks. The dry, dusty leaves added their bit to the mixture. The clean scent of morning dew clinging to cotton stalks, dried-up flower beds, feed stacks, making little diamond beads in the early sunlight, gave a piquancy to the beginning of a fall day. Color, smells, crisp weather and jewel-blue skies blended into a harmonious autumn.

A cotton field, when the bolls were hanging full and white, was a beautiful sight, something a farmer could be proud to look upon. When the cotton was at this stage Uncle would begin to worry if the good weather would hold and whether the "hands" would come to pick our crop.

We hired Mexican migrants to pick our cotton. We did not call them migrants — they were the hands who came to pick our field and then move on to pick further north in another county. We treated them fairly with kindness and respect; they treated us the same way. There was a mutual friendliness and trust between us. There was no governmental intervention nor union to negotiate our contract — it was done on a handshake.

The same family came to us year after year, a gentle, happy family. There were usually twelve or fourteen in the group counting the grandmother who came along to cook and look after any small children in the family. One of the older men spoke English and was the one in charge of the arrangements. He kept the pickers working, weighed the sacks of cotton as they were pulled to the wagon, recorded and collected wages at the end of the day. One of the agreements was that they would be paid at the end of each day. This caused Uncle some apprehension that they may decide to quietly move out in the middle of the night and leave him with a partly picked crop. But this never happened; they always stayed until the last boll was picked. They were housed in a large tent which we provided and used a cook tent they brought along. Some of the younger men rolled up in blankets and slept on the ground outside the tent. They were perfectly content with this arrangement.

We did not always have advance notice they were coming. Some years Uncle would receive a short letter — one page, often just one sentence — "Will come to pick cotton." Other years he was left in suspense — would they or would they not come? As the days passed and his anxiety grew, he walked the floor in frustration. He would shout to Auntie, "I don't know how I will get this crop in! Where will I get hands!" as if Auntie were withholding information. Then when he was beyond bearing it any longer, they would appear. Down the county road that ran in front of our house we would first see a cloud of dust and soon their old truck, loaded with an assortment of adults, children and household items, would come clearly into view. Then they were in our yard, jumping off the truck, chattering their Mexican/English greetings, wide smiles showing their perfect white teeth and brown hands reaching out to shake ours. They were more than hands; they were friends.

Uncle would relax in the comfortable confusion and hustle and bustle of getting them settled. The sacks were ready, the wagon was in the field, the cotton scales hanging from the propped-up wagon tongue, and now there were a dozen pickers eager and ready to begin first thing tomorrow morning.

There was a little girl my age and as soon as they arrived we shyly began to renew our friendship. She could not speak English; I could not speak her language, but we had our own system of communicating which was very satisfactory. Playing dolls is done the same way in any language and mud pies are made by an international recipe. Auntie would caution me, "Don't put your head next to hers for she might have head lice." However, she was always neat and clean and I'm quite sure, in the course of playing together, I put my head close to hers many times.

A picker pulled a long sack between two rows of cotton, picking bolls from the stalks on either side of him, his hands moving fast as lightning, filling the sack. The sacks were made from heavy ducking. They were about two and a half feet wide and seven feet long with a strap at the top made from a double layer of the ducking and quilted together so it stayed in place. This strap fit over the left shoulder and allowed the sack to fall open at the top so it was easy for the picker to thrust handfuls of cotton into the sack. When the sack was so full he could barely pull it down the row, he pulled it to the wagon where it was weighed, recorded in the record book and emptied into the wagon.

The sideboards were up on the wagon so it would hold enough cotton to produce, when ginned, a bale of cotton weighing between four-hundred-fifty to five hundred pounds. When the wagon was full and piled as high as possible beyond the top of the sideboards, Uncle hitched a pair of our mules to it and hauled it to the Ragtown gin. An empty wagon was put in place to be filled while he was gone.

Sometime I would awake early in the morning and hear the muffled, rhythmic creak of the wagon and the clomp of the mules' feet on the drive leading to the road. Tumbling out of bed, I'd run to my bedroom window to watch it leave. In the eerie light of the low-hanging moon I could see Uncle hunched in the front of the wagon and looming up behind him the high pile of cotton, a canvas tarpaulin covering it so it wouldn't leave a trail of cotton along the roadway. It was important to get to the gin early and get into the long line of farmers already there waiting their turn to pull their wagons under the chute. Even leaving in the wee hours of the morning, if it was a good crop year, it would be afternoon before Uncle would get back home. By that time there would be another wagonload ready for him to haul to the gin. He would leave as soon as he switched teams, letting the tired mules rest. Auntie met him at the gate and handed up a lard bucket she had packed with good things to eat. Stashing it at his feet he called "geddup" to the mules, gently tapping them with the leather lines, and they were off. Long after dark when Auntie and I were in bed, we heard the empty wagon rattling up the drive, the snort of the mules as they neared the gate and the soft welcome nicker of the pair waiting in the barn lot.

There were cotton buyers at the gin and as soon as a bale came on to the ramp and the farmer claimed it, he was made an offer to buy. If the price was right the farmer sold on the spot but if it was not, he hauled his bale home, stacked it with his other bales, and held them until the market went up. Sometime this was not such a good gamble; the market plunged instead, in which case the farmer suffered the loss. There were seed buyers, too.

Uncle kept most of our seed for it was good to mix into the cow feed and for other uses around the farm.

On these busy days Auntie and I did the evening chores. It was a rare farm woman who, when it was necessary, was not capable of taking over with the same ability as the man of the house. So on these busy harvest days we milked the cows, threw out hay for the farm animals, gathered the eggs, slopped the hogs and saw that gates and doors were closed and everything safely tucked in for the night.

Large families gathered their own crops and to accommodate this necessity school would let out for two or three weeks as soon as crops were ready to pick. If some family needed the children held out longer than the designated time to finish gathering the crop, these days were excused absences. This was a nice vacation time for me in the '20s for I was still a small child, too small to do anything except get in the way of busy men and women. Some years the crop was so poor that there was little cotton to be picked and we could not afford to have our Mexicans come. On these years, after I was older, I worked along with Auntie and Uncle. I knew from experience what it was like to pull a heavy cotton sack down a row hour after hour, have sore hands from the burrs on the bolls which stuck through the canvas gloves I wore, and sore knees from walking on them when my back grew too tired to stoop over to reach the bolls. It was not an easy job. However, the cotton crop was the money crop and very important to a farm family, so none of us complained about the hard work.

When the last wagonload had been hauled to the gin, the pickers pulled their truck onto the county road, possessions and family hanging on precariously as they waved goodbye, a cloud of dust following them out of sight. It was then Uncle could breathe that sigh of relief he had been holding in since spring when he planted the seeds; relax in a feeling of self-satisfied repleteness for a job well done. The victory was his; he had won the battle with wind, weather and unexpected hazards.

Supper that night would be a gala occasion. Auntie would cook her good buttermilk pancakes — each one as round as our plate and doused with butter and sorghum syrup. Uncle would make jokes and tease Auntie and me. When he'd finished off his last bite of pancake and pushed back his chair, he'd chuckle and say, "I just might lay in bed 'till sunup in the morning."

Next in importance to gathering the cotton crop was harvesting the row crops, for they were the main source of feed for the farm animals. All farms in those days had three or four cows to produce milk for the family, a team of mules or horses to work the fields, hogs to provide meat for the table and some to sell, and chickens to lay eggs for eating and for selling. So the row crops were planned and tended with great care.

Mr. Morris, one of our neighbors, had a feed binder and did a brisk business cutting the row crops for those farmers who did not own one. He always cut ours. The machine, pulled by a team of horses, cut the stalks off a few inches above the ground, gathered them into a bundle, secured it with a length of binder twine, tied and dropped it behind in the row. An amazing machine! The bundles were allowed to lie in the field until the sun dried and cured them before they were stacked into shocks which looked like shaggy wigwams. A field covered with hundreds of golden shocks was picturesque, much like the pictures we see in autumn issues of farm magazines. After they had seasoned, and there was time to do so, the bundles were thrown onto a wagon, hauled to the farmyard and stored in long, compact stacks. If a stack was properly laid it would turn away water and snow and withstand the strongest wind. One thing Uncle positively forbade was anyone climbing on his feed stacks; no cavorting, adventuresome kids were going to disturb his tightly laid bundles.

Cutting maize was another harvesting job. Maize grows about waist-high to a tall farmer and produces a fat head of red grain at the top of each stalk. It is good feed for cattle, pigs and chickens. The cutters walked along beside the wagon, cutting off the heads and tossing them into the wagon. Sideboards were attached to one side of the wagon, serving as a backdrop, so that a heavy-handed cutter would not throw the maize heads over the wagon instead of into it. A pair of mules was hitched to the wagon with the harness lines tied to the brake handle so that all the guidance they required was the spoken command "geddup" to move forward a space then told "whoa" to stop them. This was so the farmer could walk along beside the wagon and have his hands free to cut. Two or three people could cut maize at one wagon, using for a cutting tool a sharp-bladed Barlow knife. The chaff that blew from the heads stung and itched wherever it found a place to settle so the glove cuffs were pinned up over the shirtsleeve cuffs and a large handkerchief was knotted tightly about the neck over the shirt collar. Nothing stung worse than chaff down a sweaty neck or on bare wrists. When the wagon was full of heads it was hauled to the barn and dumped into the maize crib.

Corn was harvested the same way as the maize except the ears were pulled off the stalks. One grabbed an ear, gave it a twist and a sharp whack with the heel of the hand and off it came. Our corncrib was a separate small building and stood near the chicken house east of the cow barn. This was the usual location for the crib, or near the hog pen, for the hogs and chickens consumed most of the crop.

Because Halloween was likely to come during cotton-picking season I can recall only one time when we celebrated it with a big school party. In fact, not much was made of Halloween except for the pictures we drew at school of jack-o-lanterns, ghosts and witches on their brooms. Ghost stories were read sometime during the day in some of the classrooms. We had never heard of trick-or-treat. If it was a bright moonlit night the older kids might get out in a group and play tricks around the community. It never could be anything very big because all the farms had watchdogs that set up to barking when anything out of the ordinary came on the place. And if a farmer owned a flock of guineas the kids gave his place a wide berth. There is no known sentinel better than a flock of guineas; they have a sixth sense about any stranger — man or beast — being about and set to "pot-racking" so furiously that there is no question about what one should do.

It was on one of those years when we had a poor crop and the picking season was cut short that we had this big, memorable school party. Parents and children alike welcomed the celebration as a refreshing break from the monotony of fall field work.

A lot of excitement surrounded preparation for the big

night. The older students turned one of the upstairs rooms into a spook house; each classroom was responsible for a game, prank or trick. We spent every spare minute the week before planning, making decorations and collecting props for our games and fun. On Halloween night, in the light of the kerosene lamps, the desks and blackboards took on a strange and eerie appearance festooned with bundles of hay, cornstalks and pumpkins. The mothers were much in evidence, bustling about, setting up their table where they served cookies, popcorn balls and lemonade. The fathers stood leaning against the walls discussing how many bales of cotton their crop had produced and the price cotton buyers were paying, how many stacks of hay they stood to feed the farm animals until another crop could be made and harvested, and what hogs were selling for — all the time keeping a sharp eye out for any over-excited boys who seemed bent on making mischief.

Our costumes were contrived from whatever we could find in the scrap bag or storage chest at home. There were lots of ghosts and tramps. It was a fun night — laughter, fortune-telling by one of the clever mothers dressed like a gypsy, screams from girls as they made a tour of the spook house (where the older girls were draped in sheets and had us feel the "bones and blood and eyes of the vampire"), hoots from the boys who hid around corners and jumped out at unsuspecting girls, lots of horseplay and eating and youthful pranks. We relived it all the next day as we cleaned up our classrooms, erasing all traces of the night's revelry, and into the next week as we remembered the scares we shared and the tricks we played on each other.

Time came when the last bale of cotton had been sold

and the money was safely in the bank. The maize and cornstalks had been cut to lie in the fields and be plowed under next spring. Once again the endless miles of farmland lay brown and barren. A quiet urgency took hold, a hush, as we prepared for the first cold day.

WINTER

By late November the weather had taken a sharp turn toward winter. The wind had begun to assert itself, driving the cold into one's body like a sharp knife. Even the south wind had lost any vestige of warmth.

When the wind blew straight out of the north we called it a norther. Northers were uncomfortable to deal with, often bringing blue-black clouds which looked fiercely down upon us as they hurried across the sky, cutting off the sun. When it blew like this we called it a blue norther. Any norther was cold, but a blue norther was almost unbearable. It came on a normal winter day, quietly and unobtrusively, unnoticed, until we looked north, about mid-morning, and saw a dark, very blue rim above the horizon. As the rim rose to cover the sky the wind scattered it into ominous, threatening clouds, and together they produced miserable weather. Out of doors the numbing cold cut through our layers of clothing straight to the bone — bone chilling.

There were probably colder climates than West Texas winters back in the '20s but it would have been hard to convince any West Texan of this possibility. But weather was faced and endured like any other unavoidable condition, without complaint. We swung from one season to the next, doing whatever was necessary at that time to sustain us, our farm animals and day-to-day living. We lived very much in the present, following the natural pattern of events. If the weather was cold — well, winter was supposed to be cold. So, far in advance of the first hard cold spell, we did what one would logically expect to do — attend to certain essential preparations that would keep ourselves and the animals as comfortable as possible.

If there was such a thing as insulation for walls and windows we certainly had never heard of it in our part of the country. So we made our own. Auntie folded the *Semi-Weekly News* (which she saved and used in numerous ways) and pressed them between the sashes of all the windows; this served admirably to keep out cold drafts. The window cooler, so important for keeping food cool in summer, served no useful function in winter so it was covered with ducking to keep the cold air out of the kitchen.

Water pipes were a factor to deal with. The pipe that came down from the overhead storage tank was housed in a wood casing which was filled with sawdust or cotton seed, but the pipes supplying water to the house and the water trough in the barnyard were not so well protected.

This meant the cutoff beneath the storage tank must be checked to make sure it was in good working order, for one of the cardinal rules in winter was: turn off the water as soon as evening chores were finished. During very cold spells the water was cut off during the daytime, too, turning it on from time to time to run a bucketful for cooking and drinking.

The isinglass curtains had to be put on the sides of the Model-T touring car. Hung on the garage wall through the summer months, the isinglass had become dry and brittle so that it was easily cracked and broken. It would take Auntie the better part of a day to replace the broken "windows" with new isinglass. This done, she and Uncle had the tedious chore of fitting each curtain to the proper door and fastening it down with the turn keys mounted on the door facings inside the car. Henceforth, until spring, every time a person got in or out of the car the part attached to the door had to be unfastened and held up above the head so the passenger could get out. It was not possible to accomplish this feat gracefully; it was rather more like an athletic contest. More times than not a brisk wind snatched the curtain from one's grasp. An impulsive, frantic lunge was the normal reaction to save it before the isinglass window was broken — at the same time clinging doggedly to an armful of books and a lunch pail, or purse and parcel, depending upon one's age and station in life. Be it noted that the wind, during this frenzied activity, has grasped the opportunity to blow one's clothing every which way, and if one had neatly done homework, to scatter it to the sky. But curtains did add considerable comfort to traveling on a cold winter's day.

Setting up the heating stove in the front room was one

of winter's most important preparations. Putting up the stove was as exacting, if not more so, than taking it down in the spring.

The first and easiest step was bringing it from the maize crib where it had been stored through the summer months, gathering a thick coating of maize dust, and setting it upright in the backyard where it underwent a thorough cleaning. It was polished with a special black liquid which gave off a peculiar smell the first time a fire was built and the chrome decoration was vigorously rubbed until it shone like new. Not until the finished job met with Auntie's approval was it ready for the next step on its journey for we, and everyone who came to see us, would be seeing it all winter. Nothing short of perfection was acceptable. This accomplished, it must be carried up the back steps and through the kitchen door — not as simple as it may sound. It was a heavy, clumsy piece, awkward to handle, with no really good spot to get a handhold.

Uncle would instruct Auntie, "You get at the front and walk up the steps and I'll bear the weight from behind." This much brought them to the top step and the open door — Auntie standing just inside, holding on for dear life. The stove, relaxed as only a hulk of iron could be, grinned through its front openings expecting to enjoy the struggle. Uncle stood on the step below, every muscle straining to hold it upright. "Now, I'll push and you guide it through the door," Uncle would say, with doubtful optimism. After several attempts, Auntie would say, "Let me get at the back and you guide it through." He would continue to hold on to the stove while Auntie went out the front door and around the house to the back steps. She put all her body force against it while he made the trip around the house to take her place. After several fruitless attempts the only noticeable change was that patience was wearing thin with both parties. Stress and strain were taking their toll.

So they exchanged positions again; Uncle at the back to push and Auntie at the front to guide. "Mr. Mangum, quit pushing so hard! You push and I lose my hold and we'll drop it!" "Just how, Madam, do you expect to get this stove through the door if I don't push?" "Hold it in place and I'll pull!" This method did not work either.

The opening was barely wide enough for the stove to slip through and it seemed to grow smaller as their efforts came to nothing. Positioning it perfectly was the key and one of the deterrents to this key was the decorative chrome rim that ran around its circumference — too rounded at the bottom to be used as a handhold but wide enough to cause trouble. It was causing trouble now. "Maybe if I lift it and pull at the same time?" Auntie offered. "No! No! Set it down! Hold on! Just see if you can keep it from falling on top of me!" Uncle, in total exasperation, would finally put his shoulder against it and give a great push. By now tempers had reached the boiling point. "You pushed too hard! The rim is caught!" "Next spring we are leaving this thing in the house," Uncle would declare just as the stove neatly slipped through the door as if it were the easiest task in the world. It was negotiated through one more door and settled into its final resting place in exact alignment with the chimney opening at the top of the north living-room wall.

After the trauma of setting the stove in place, fitting the pipes together was a breeze. There were three black, shiny sections: a straight-up piece that fit into an opening on top of the stove, a curved section with accordion-like ridges, and a second straight piece that lay between the curved section and the chimney opening. However, there was one more hazardous hurdle to be cleared — to remove, very carefully, the metal cover from the chimney opening. Through the summer months soot had sifted down from inside the chimney and, at all cost, it must not be allowed to drift out into the room and to settle upon lace curtains, wallpaper and wood floors. This was Auntie's job because by now Uncle was too nervous to handle such a delicate operation. Then the final act of placing the pipe into the opening. Ah! The job was done; mission accomplished; the sigh of relief.

Throughout this long and colorful procedure I kept quietly and unobtrusively in the background — just close enough to savor the drama of the situation but far enough away to stay out of the line of fire. The function of taking down and putting up the heating stove was performed twice yearly on a regular basis so it seems, as efficient as they both were, Auntie and Uncle would have figured out a workable formula. But this was never accomplished — it was a new experience each time and, from all I could find out from my friends, typical for most households.

If Uncle could afford to do so he would lay in a supply of feed for the cows to last through the winter months. Cows needed more nourishment in cold weather when there was no pasture to graze. One of the main food supplies was a feed mixture made from grain grown on the farm and ground at Mr. Thomas' mill. Besides the home-ground mixture there were sacks of bran and a delicious-smelling sticky mixture bought in town at Williams Feed Store (which also dealt in the sale of mules and horses). The sticky mixture had molasses in it and each cow got half a coffee canful on top of her feed portion at evening milking. Probably few farm cows fared so well as Bonnie, Vita, Shanks and Lillie.

The hens and roosters must not be overlooked. The front of their house was screened to let in the cool breeze during hot weather but must be closed in for the winter. Besides the discomfort — which was a major consideration since all farm denizens were treated with respect and kindness — hens would often pout around in winter and refuse to lay eggs on a regular basis. And eggs we needed, for our own table and to sell to Mr. Childress' store. So we must give the hens the special attention they were demanding if we were to have their eggs. To handle this problem, Uncle mounted a long dowel above the screened portion and attached ducking to it so that it could be rolled down like a window shade and fastened securely at the bottom with hooks. This protection, together with their fluffed-out feathers, kept them cozy through the cold winter nights.

The plowshares were cleaned until they shone like silver, then covered with axle grease to protect them from the winter weather. Harness was repaired, oiled and hung in the harness room.

The coal bin and kerosene barrel were filled before the first cold spell. Uncle drove the wagon to town and brought back a ton of coal so that the bin was heaped to running over. We hoped it would "burn slow" since it cost eight dollars and fifty cents a ton. A truck from the Day and Night Garage delivered the kerosene to fill our yellow fifty-five-gallon barrel which was mounted on a platform inside the backyard.

There was activity inside the house, too. Flannel blankets replaced summer sheets on the beds. Winter clothing was taken out of storage and hung on the clothesline so wind and sun would clear out the odor of mothballs. I was required to try on my wool dresses and skirts and my coat to see if hems could be let out and sleeves lengthened to get another winter's wear from them. Auntie was clever about adding a new collar or buttons or trim to give a dress a fresh look, but so were all farm mothers. Turning a garment was common practice. A sharp ripper was necessary for this job; one pair of hands held the garment while another carefully cut the threads to open the seams. The seams were pressed open and the inside of the fabric turned to the outside and the seams resewn. Presto! All shiny, damaged spots disappeared to the underside and the garment looked like a new one.

In the cold months Auntie and Uncle would "do up the work" early in the evening before the sun dropped too low in the sky, while there was still some sunshine left to take the edge off the cold. While Uncle threw bundles of hay to the mules, Auntie would measure out feed into the trough under each cow's stanchion so they could eat while they were being milked. While they did the milking I was going from hen nest to hen nest gathering the eggs that had been laid that day.

The hogs were fed, at any season, after the milk was brought into the kitchen and put through the separator. First, Auntie filled a large stone jar with whole milk; no "bluejohn" was ever seen on our table — we drank rich, sweet, full-bodied milk. After the thick, yellow cream was separated out, the bluejohn that was left was carried to the hog pen and poured into their trough for it was not considered fit for anything else. The hogs loved it, squealing contentedly as they fought over a place at the trough.

While Auntie was occupied with attending to the milk, Uncle shut the hen house door, checked the animals to see that all was well with them, brought in an extra scuttle of coal and sufficient kindling to start a fire in the heating stove the next morning. The last security measure for the night, after the separator was washed and put away, was to draw a large bucket of water at the kitchen sink so Uncle could cut off the water outside at the storage tank, making sure all pipes leading to the house were drained.

If the car had been driven that day the water had to be drained from the radiator; otherwise, there might be a frozen block next morning, a devastating discovery. For good measure an old quilt was thrown over the hood. Starting a Model-T on a cold morning was a frustrating challenge without adding possible catastrophe. Often Uncle poured a kettle of hot water over the block before he tried to crank the motor.

In other seasons we ate for supper what was left over from dinner or a bowl of Post Toasties but cold weather called for a hot meal. Auntie set before us steaming bowls of cornmeal mush or rice to which we added cream, butter and sugar, or she made big, fluffy pancakes that covered our plates, lavishly enhanced with melted butter and sorghum syrup. This tasted very good, consumed near the warmth of the cookstove, knowing the animals and water pipes were secure for the night. The only thorn left to mar these cozy-comfort thoughts was knowing there was a long, cold walk to the outdoor privy before going to bed.

After supper we found our special places in the front room by the heating stove. Uncle propped back in his cane-bottomed chair beside the table where the lighted lamp stood and read the *Semi-Weekly News* or the *Farm & Ranch Magazine.*

The *Semi-Weekly News*, widely read by country folk, was published in Dallas and delivered to us twice weekly by our mail carrier. The front page headlined the state, national and worldwide news. It told us what the governor, congressmen and the president of the United States were in conflict over; the crisis we were experiencing or could expect to experience. The news affected us very much as it does today except for one distinct difference. By the time the word reached us — coming out of Dallas by way of train, overnight in the post office at Post, another day to process and place it in the hands of our rural mail carrier who had yet to deliver it to our box — it was too late to worry over the bad news.

The paper contained interesting features for all the family. There was a serialized romance or western story which Auntie eagerly reached for, a farm page that told Uncle what price he could expect to receive for his cotton crop and hogs and described any new wrinkle farmers were experimenting with in other parts of the country and suggestions that might make his work easier or crops more productive. There was a woman's page with household hints, a dress pattern to order, quilt and embroidery patterns. For the children there was an ongoing story called "Uncle Wiggly." There were no comics nor crossword nor acrostic puzzles but usually a funny cartoon and a regular column on the order of Erma Bombeck called "Aunt Hannah." Heading up this column was a drawing of a woman in a poke bonnet smoking a pipe.

Farm & Ranch Magazine came once a month and had similar features to the *Semi-Weekly* but without news items and with farm and home articles in more depth. It, too, had a children's page.

Besides these regular publications, Auntie "took" *Delineator* and *Woman's Home Companion*. Both covered all the subjects dear to a woman's heart — self-improvement articles, love stories, dress designs, recipes, beautiful colored advertisements and for the delight of little girls there was a page of Dolly Dingle paper dolls.

When kitchen chores were done we joined Uncle in the front room bringing with us the kitchen lamp to add light to the lamp already setting on the table. Auntie liked the other side of the table from Uncle to do her handwork or to read. I'd take the Sears Roebuck and Montgomery Ward mail order catalogs from the shelf under the library table and lose myself in the magic of their multitude of products, turning from page to page, making my pretend selections. They were the shopping malls of the '20s; a country woman's shopping paradise. Anything the heart desired could be found among their pages — perfume to horse collars, handkerchiefs to tents, sewing thread to buggies or a Model-T Ford; from Sears one could order a house; all kinds of clothing for men, women and children; dishes, sheets, clothes wringers, cooking utensils; laces, fabric, pins and needles; songbooks, organs, bird cages, corsets — just think of the article and it could be found in either catalog. All one had to do to make a purchase was fill out one of the enclosed order blanks, attach a personal check or money order, affix a two-cent stamp to the addressed envelope and put it in the mailbox in front of the house with the flag up. In a few days your package arrived along with the assurance that if you were not satisfied with the merchandise you could return it and your money would be refunded.

After awhile Auntie would disappear into the kitchen and come back with the dishpan filled with fresh popped corn. We three would eat the whole thing! This corn had been grown on the farm. Uncle had planted and gathered it and I had shelled it by rubbing two ears against each other. A slow process but well worth the effort when it was popped on a winter's night and eaten by the light of a lamp, in the warmth of a red-hot heating stove.

At ten o'clock it was time to prepare for bed — something not anticipated with much pleasure. The only heated rooms in the house were the kitchen, which was warm when Auntie was cooking a meal, and the front room where the black-iron heating stove was located. The doors leading from these rooms into the bedrooms were kept closed in order to contain what heat we could generate in the area where we spent most of our time. Going into my bedroom was like a trip to the North Pole. In the light of the lamp the furnishings looked brittle and forbidding and the bed was an enemy to be conquered and then endured. We were well dressed for the occasion, however. Long before cold weather set in Auntie had made long cotton flannel nightgowns for herself and me with nightcaps to match, and she had crocheted bedslippers from wool thread which fit our feet like socks. Uncle slept in his union suit and wool socks.

When it was time to dress for bed, Uncle, in mutual respect for our modesty, turned his back to me so I could change into my night clothes in the cozy circle of heat around the stove. With my flannel gown on, my nightcap tied under my chin and bedslippers snug on my feet, I'd make a dash for my bed and dive under the covers into its miserably cold discomfort.

My bed was well prepared. There was a cotton flannel double blanket which I slept next to. It was called "double" because the top and bottom was one continuous piece so that it was not possible to have one's feet uncovered. The next item was a wool quilt Auntie had pieced and quilted from blocks made from good parts of worn-out garments. On top of this quilt were spread as many others as necessary, adding more as the nights grew colder. Even lying under such a pile, I would shiver until my body heat created a warm spot, after which I did not dare move a muscle, not even a little toe. On the coldest nights Auntie would heat a sadiron on top of the stove, wrap it in a towel and put it to my feet which kept me warm until I went to sleep.

The first sound I heard in the morning was Uncle shaking the ashes from the stove grate. I'd hear him open the stove to lay a bed of kindling and pour on a small amount of kerosene so the flame would catch quickly, then lay on a good supply of coal. Soon I would hear the roar of the fire and know it would not be long until Uncle called me to get up. When he did, I'd get quickly out of bed, dash across the icy bedroom floor and into the welcome warmth of the front room to dress for school. On winter mornings we schoolgirls did not mind the layers of clothing we were required to wear and even welcomed the unpopular union suit, not caring too much that it made our bodies look lumpy and ungainly.

A large black stove stood in a corner of each schoolroom and a fire had been going in it since early morning. The warmth was a welcome comfort to half-frozen school kids who came puffing into the room with red noses and frosty breath. Some students walked as far as four miles, the harsh wind cutting through their coats and the frozen ground making their feet numb. Uncle drove me to school in the car. The wind blew through the openings between the curtains across the car doors, and the cold air rushed up through the cracks in the wooden floorboard. I was only a little less cold than those who walked; I just did not have to endure it as long as they did.

Thanksgiving preparation was begun well in advance of the day, for it was celebrated with the pomp and ceremony it deserved. All the parents and children in the Ragtown community gathered on Thanksgiving morning in the school auditorium to see the program the students had prepared and practiced and for which the mothers had provided costumes.

The program was opened as the assembled parents and students stood to sing "America" — with more zeal than tune — from the *Golden Book of Songs*, accompanied on the piano by one of the teachers. One of the school orators, picked from the upper grades, gave the main address, expressing the seriousness of our celebration, a day to be honored with grateful hearts, remembering the hardships and sacrifice of our Pilgrim Fathers. This was followed by a chorus from the upper grades, and then came the part we all liked best, the recitation of the poem, "Over the River and Through the Woods." The final piece was the play put on by the lower grades, enacting the landing of the Pilgrims and the first Thanksgiving feast. We performed our parts with gravity, feeling the responsibility of appropriately portraying our forefathers and the founding of our country. The seriousness of our intent was hampered somewhat, however, since having waited so long to perform our part we'd had time to develop a case of jittery nerves and the Indians, in their scanty clothes, delivered their lines through chattering teeth. But, all in all, the performance rose to the occasion and we felt proud of ourselves as the applause rolled across the auditorium.

As soon as Mr. Robinson declared the program at an end, the meeting quickly broke up. Mothers were eager to get back to the kitchen and fathers and children were ready for the feast and fellowship with friends and relatives that awaited them at home.

At our house plenty of cooks were left at home to prepare the dinner, so delicious smells greeted us as we returned, cold and hungry, from our morning activity. Grandma, Grandpa and Aunt Mattie had arrived with Aunt Rosa and Uncle Bob, who had come the day before from Gorman, almost two hundred miles away. Other aunts and uncles and cousins had come from the adjoining county so we had a gathering befitting the occasion.

For this special dinner leaves had been added to the dining table to open up to its longest size. Auntie had set it with the white embroidered cloth and our nicest dishes; neatly folded napkins were laid at each place and the glass serving bowls were brought from the cupboard.

Dish after dish of steaming food was brought to the table — a plump baked hen resting on a platter and surrounded with mounds of corn-bread dressing, giblet gravy, mashed potatoes, candied sweet potatoes, green beans (canned, from last summer's garden), apple and raisin salad, beet pickles, peach pickles with cloves pushed into their meaty sides, chow-chow, biscuits, pumpkin and mince pies — at least three of each — and sitting smack in the middle of the table on Grandma's cut-glass cake stand was a four-layer chocolate cake that Aunt Mattie had baked. This was not all; there were backups in the kitchen — a roast of beef and sliced home-cured ham and store-bought loaves of bread. No one went hungry on Thanksgiving Day.

The grown-ups spent the afternoon visiting. The men sat in the front room discussing how good, or poor, their harvest had been, the price of cattle and hogs, politics and telling stories of days gone by. The women gathered in the kitchen or one of the bedrooms to exchange family gossip, look at handwork and quilts, trade recipes and talk about the days that used to be. The children played games in one of the bedrooms or the kitchen, depending upon where the women had chosen to gather. We played I spy and blindman's bluff mixed with a good portion of squabbling, heated arguments over rules and accusations of peeking. If we grew too rambunctious we were "called down." If weather permitted, we played outside and then it didn't matter how noisy we were. One of our favorite outdoor games was Annie over, in which players in the front yard threw a ball over the house to the players in the backyard. It was more complicated than it appears to be, for it involved tagging the opposing team members if the ball was caught without hitting the ground; things could grow very noisy and competitive. Our house was perfectly designed for such a game since it had a simple gable roof. The ball hit the roof a lot so the game lasted until the adults got tired of the thump-thump and made us stop. We'd finish the day with hide-and-go-seek, which we never tired of playing.

It was a good day of fun, feasting and fellowship; a day spent with family and close friends creating lasting memories.

By Monday we were back in school. Long holidays were neither necessary nor desirable, for school was a major part of our social life. We had a recess at mid-morning and again at mid-afternoon, then an hour recess at noon so there was plenty of time to play, share together, build relationships and work out our differences and quarrels — a social interchange that was a rich part of our learning experience. There was a sense of comradeship, tempered with keen competition in our classrooms as we shared lessons, competed in spelling bees, speaking contests and report-card grades. A special rapport grew out of our joint efforts preparing for school functions and celebrations. In those years the social life of the farm community was centered around the school and the church. Not very exciting but quite satisfactory.

Farm folk out in West Texas in the 1920s let events ebb and flow and come into being at an unhurried, uncluttered pace. Christmas being no exception, it marched to its own rhythm, systematically and satisfactorily reaching a climax on Christmas Day. There was no two-month buildup with decorations, gift reminders and commercials hitting us full in the face right on the heels of Halloween. There was very little commercialization in those years to distract us, particularly not in the farming communities on the West Texas plains. December was the month of Christmas and not much mention was made of it before that time.

The religious significance of the season was not emphasized over any other part of the holiday. Christmas was shared equally between Jesus and Santa Claus and the distinction between the two was clearly understood.

The first visible sign of Christmas, which signaled the opening of the season, was the appearance of toys in the stores in town, usually the first or second Saturday in the month. Celluloid dolls, tops, marbles, jacks, balls and other trifles could be bought any time through the year in Doughty's Racket Store but other toys were available only at the Christmas season. For this momentous event Bryant Link set up a toy section as did Stevens Dry Goods but best of all was the basement at Greenfield's Hardware Store.

147

Greenfield's had a broad wooden stairway leading down to their basement — a novelty in and of itself. The door at the head of the stairs was opened only at the Christmas season when the room below was filled with toys. To walk down that stairway, holding on to the banister with one hand and Auntie's hand with the other, and see the kaleidoscope of toys spread below was like walking into an enchanted kingdom. There were brightly colored rocking horses, dolls with real hair, dressed in frilly dresses and bonnets, wicker doll carriages, little china tea sets, all sizes of red wagons, tricycles, balls, a shelf of books, folders of paper dolls, black iron play stoves, little tin utensils — and more.

We country kids drifted through this wonderful dreamland touching and trying as we wandered from toy to toy. Dolls were lifted off the shelf to be cuddled in eager arms, hands stroking the silky material of the dress. The wagons had to be tested; the teapot lifted by its minute handle and the cups inspected. Gun barrels had to be looked down and triggers pulled, pocketknives opened and tested for sharpness. Puzzles inspected. The bookshelf was invaded by curious hands feeling the smooth newness of the pages. Usually one of the store clerks would "wind up" a train and we'd all gather to watch the engine chug around the circular track pulling the painted tin cars. Tricycles were a popular item as we took advantage of the rare opportunity for riding one. None of us owned one since rough, uneven yards were not appropriate for riding tricycles.

One Christmas the toy basement held something special, so unique and wonderful I was immediately, totally captivated. It was on a Saturday about two weeks before Christmas that Auntie, Uncle and I were in town and went by Greenfield's to see the toys. As we walked down the basement stairs I saw sitting in the midst of all the other toys a yellow desk and chair. Dropping Auntie's hand, I flew down the steps and, like a homing pigeon, went straight to the chair and sat down. It was just right. Carefully I moved my hands over the shiny desk top, lifting it to inspect the space beneath where Crayolas, pencils, paper and books could be stored. With the top down it slanted just right for propping a book or tablet or slate. It was obvious, without my saying so for the tenth time, that I had set my heart on having the desk and chair. Throughout the days ahead it was never out of my mind. I daydreamed about it, pretended it was in my room.

When we were in town on Christmas Eve I asked to go to Greenfield's. All the way down the basement stairs my eyes were searching for the coveted desk and chair but they were nowhere to be seen. Frantically I pushed through the crowd, looking; searching for the item of my heart's desire. In and among the trains and dolls, the blocks and buggies I hunted but it was not to be found. The yellow desk and chair were gone. My joy and anticipation, my staunch, unwavering belief in Santa Claus and his reindeer turned to a bitter ache in my throat. The disappointment was too keen for tears. When we reached the sidewalk outside on the street, the happy hustle and bustle and the noisy popping firecrackers were like a mockery. Christmas seemed lost and gone and faraway — it had disappeared before it had ever happened.

"I want to go home," I said to Auntie.

"Home! Why, we have hardly done anything," she answered.

"I feel sick," I said. And I was sick. Homesick to go home where familiarity would warm the cold ashes of my heart.

I don't remember what happened the rest of that Christmas Eve, but I do remember clearly on Christmas morning opening the door between my bedroom and the front room and standing too astonished to speak or move, for there beside the heating stove stood the yellow desk and chair. Scrooge, in his miraculous discovery on Christmas morning that he was alive and could redeem himself, could not have felt more pure, indescribable joy than I felt at that moment. Never again would I doubt Santa Claus, and I have not to this good day!

As if on cue, on the Monday following the appearance of toys in the stores, we walked into our schoolroom to find Miss Bond had drawn a large Santa Claus on one end of the blackboard and colored it with red chalk. It would remain there until after the holidays — only a villain would have dared touch it or erase any part of it.

Lying on our desks were sheets of red and green construction paper. In the week that followed, the sheets were converted into endless yards of paper chains which were strung around the room, and bells, trees and wreaths which were stuck on the window panes. Since Scotch tape had not yet been invented, it is a miracle how they stayed on the panes, but whatever the method, it worked. All the grade-school classrooms were similarly decorated by busy and eager hands, which served to intensify our merriment and anticipation.

One of the events which caused a good deal of discussion, before and after the fact, was the drawing of names. Each student wrote his or her name on a slip of paper, folded it and placed it in a box. The box was passed down the aisles and each child drew out a name. The name you drew was the classmate for whom you would bring a gift to be placed under the school Christmas tree. The gifts were not elegant nor costly nor beautifully wrapped. Mostly, they were handmade or some trinket from Doughty's or something from home that a parent could be talked into parting with. But they were exciting to receive and it was fun to find out who had drawn your name. The names were to be kept secret but this rule was not strictly observed. Often changes were negotiated. Once Irene Hawthorne, a special friend, traded her Crayolas for my name, a show of affection which incurred real sacrifice on her part, for Crayolas were not easily come by. Her gift to me was a little china doll which, to my grief, was lost somewhere down the years. In most cases it was easy to tell whether a "drawer" was pleased or displeased with his or her name. Not everyone was like Lucile Meador who would carefully unfold the slip of paper, peep at the name, fold it back again and place it in her pencil box. That would be the last we would see, or know, of her name until the gifts were handed out. More often there were moans and declarations from those who were displeased, saying they would not bring a gift to such a person! Others were so pleased with their name they smirked their satisfaction and refused to tell anyone who it was. I was strictly instructed at home that I was neither to reveal nor trade the name I drew, regardless of who it was.

One day, soon after the school Christmas activities began, when I arrived home from school and turned through the gate I'd see green wreaths hanging in the front room windows. Inside, the familiar decorations would be in place and a delicious spicy smell coming from the kitchen. My heartbeat quickened. Here was concrete evidence that Christmas was just around the corner.

Our decorations were very simple but to a little country

girl they were beautiful. A big red bell made of tissue paper hung from the center of the front room ceiling. The bell closed down flat when stored away but when opened up it blossomed out like a huge honeycomb. Green woven paper ropes were attached above the bell and swooped in graceful arches to each corner of the room. A green wreath with a bright red bow hung in each window. Few, if any, farm homes had a tree — those were for churches and schools.

The good smell coming from the kitchen meant the baking was under way. Auntie and Aunt Mattie, singly and jointly, were now in a frenzy of preparation. Heaven only knew how many would be around the table for Christmas dinner! Even if no one came, which was highly unlikely, there must be plenty of good things to feast on, not only on the day but throughout the week between Christmas and New Year's Day.

I would be pressed into service to crack and shell nuts. Our nutcracker was a sadiron and a hammer. Very few halves came out intact with that system but it did not matter — the good taste was there. I was sent on numerous trips to the cellar to bring up apples, jars of mincemeat and other supplies stored there.

The applesauce cake was baked first then wrapped in a sugar-sack cloth and placed on the pantry shelf to grow sticky and rich with spicy flavor and aroma. Pies — mince and apple — were stored on top of the kitchen cabinet.

Making candy was the part I liked best. When Auntie made divinity I stood on a box by the cabinet and poured the hot syrup into the beaten egg whites while Auntie stirred with all her might. The sugar, water and white Karo had been boiled together until, when a small stream was poured from the tip of a spoon, it spun a long, silky thread. The dab left on the spoon was dropped into a cup of cold water, and if on contact it made a crackling sound, the syrup was ready. It must be poured very slowly in a thin stream onto the stiffly beaten egg whites. It was a tedious operation; arms ached from holding the pan and from the constant beating. But the results were worth the effort — tall, light, creamy pieces filled with nuts, the likes of which could not be bought at any price. Mexican orange candy was another delicious Christmas tradition. This required grating an orange peel, another of my chores — too often I grated my fingers on the sharp points. But, likewise, that pain was forgotten when the candy was finished and poured into a buttered platter and cut into delicious chunks. Date loaf was another favorite and there could not have been a complete holiday without it. When all was finished, these candies were placed between layers of butter papers (paper used to wrap a pound of molded butter) and stored in tin lard buckets, the lids pressed firmly into place.

Uncle did not like the dark, rich cakes so Auntie made an angel food — light as a feather — to appease his appetite. Then for good measure, and because one cannot have too many cakes at Christmas, she baked a three-layer coconut. It was richly layered together with thick creamy filling generous with coconut. The icing was a white frothy confection piled an inch thick all over the cake and covered thickly with coconut. A mouth-watering work of art.

As she did at Thanksgiving, Aunt Mattie baked her famous chocolate layer cake. Four rich yellow layers held together with velvety chocolate, thick as candy, lavishly spread between each layer and covering the entire outside. She made graceful swirls in the frosting which gave the cake a haughty appearance in keeping with its usual place of honor in the center of the dining table, grandly mounted on Grandma's cake stand.

When Aunt Mattie produced one of these cakes it was a notable undertaking. After lunch dishes were washed and put away, her apron still in place covering her dress, she let it be known — emphatically — that she wanted no one in the kitchen bothering her because she meant to make a cake. We do not know what went on during this process for we never dared set foot inside the kitchen door. We satisfied ourselves that progress was being made by listening to the rattle of pans and sniffing the good smells that escaped through the open door. Eventually, she emerged from the confines of the kitchen to announce the cake was done, but the oven hadn't heated right, the chocolate was hard to grate and the cream too thin, ending on the ominous declaration, "I'll swan, it won't be fit to eat!" But on the day it was cut and the perfect slices placed on our outstretched plates, it was discovered to be excellent beyond describing. I'll swan, it was delicious!

Aunt Rosa always brought the fruitcake which had idled away its days swathed in a brandy-soaked cloth while waiting for Christmas to arrive. The only Christmas I can remember getting sick was when I ate too much of Aunt Rosa's fruitcake.

At school the excitement was mounting day by day. It reached its peak on the day before school let out for the holidays when the tree was brought in on Mr. Dalby's truck.

It was always a cedar tree, for they grew in abundance in the little hills and ravines below the Caprock. On that morning, after the last bell had rung "to take up books," Mr. Dalby drove to the schoolhouse in his flatbed truck to pick up a half dozen of the strongest boys to go along with him to select and cut the tree. All the older boys were hoping and praying to be one of the lucky six, for it was considered to be a great lark. Besides getting out of classes and the fun of riding on the truck, they could race around over the unfamiliar draws and gullies.

Some time before school let out for the day, they would drive into the schoolyard, the tree covering the bed of the truck, its branches hanging over on both sides, for they always cut the biggest and best to be found. If the children were out for a recess, what a commotion it created! Kids ran from every corner of the grounds to get as near as possible to the tree, to marvel at its size and revel in the pungent smell. The boys, with Mr. Dalby and Mr. Robinson directing them, carried it to the auditorium on the second floor and onto the stage. The lower grades were not allowed to go upstairs except for chapel each Thursday morning and other stated occasions, so this would be our last glimpse of the tree until it was ready for the event the next afternoon.

Next morning the older students decorated the tree with ornaments they had made or brought from home. The gifts, which had been collecting in the rooms, were picked up to be placed under it. We young students were giddy with excitement. The morning was exasperatingly long and tedious. Half-heartedly we tried to keep our mind on spelling and reading and other mundane things. The noon recess, which usually sped so quickly, seemed to last forever. Finally, back in the schoolroom, sitting primly quiet but bursting inside with suppressed excitement, we heard Miss Bond give the long-awaited signal for us to rise, march single file down the corridor and up the stairs to take our accustomed seats in the auditorium.

It was a magical moment when we arrived at the top of the stairs and saw the tree in all its magnificent splendor. The handmade decorations dangled from its branches and the glittering ropes of tinsel wound about it, sparkling and twinkling from the light of the tall windows. The floor all around the tree was piled high with gifts and the green smell of cedar permeated the big room — it was a special moment for us, caught up in the wonder and thrill of the essence of Christmas.

After all the classes had marched in and were seated, Mr. Robinson stepped onto the stage, causing complete quiet and order to settle over the room, and announced we were to expect a visitor. Almost at once we heard the heavy tramp of footsteps coming up the stairs. Every head was turned as a jovial "HO-HO-HO" rang out and there on the landing stood Santa Claus. Everyone except Miss Bond's first- and second-grade room knew it was someone's father but that did not dim the splendor and magic of the red suit and the white beard.

Santa threw handfuls of candy, gum and wax dolls and dogs filled with a red, sweet strange-tasting liquid. This brought on a great scramble — the boys pushing and shoving and crawling on the floor to get as many pieces as possible. After the pandemonium died down, Santa called for some of the older girls to distribute gifts.

There was always the dread that your name would not be called, that it had been lost or tossed out or the person who drew it forgot to bring a gift. But in spite of doubt and worry and all earlier declarations, everyone received a gift. You heard your own name called and with great relief and curiosity accepted the package, sometimes wrapped in brown paper, or not wrapped at all, or in red tissue paper with sprigs of holly printed on it. West Texas kids had never seen holly but we knew from pictures and from singing about it that it was a part of Christmas. Once one of my friends brought to school a sprig of mistletoe that a relative from Arkansas had sent her. It was a curiosity but we had lots of fun with it for we knew from the poems and stories we had read how it was to be used.

Before we were dismissed we sang all the familiar carols, ending with a loud and boisterous rendition of "Jingle Bells." We parted for the holidays happily clasping our gifts, however scant or cheap, and eager for the next unfoldment of Christmas.

Christmas Eve was looked forward to more keenly than any day of the year. We were up early that morning hurrying through the preparations for going to town. The weather usually controlled whether or not we went to town or on any other outing, but on Christmas Eve it did not matter what the weather was. We went. This was the day all families went to Post to buy toys, fruit, nuts, candy and other treats for the Christmas Day festivities, so it was unthinkable that any of us would have missed the excitement and fun.

It was a merry crowd. Neighbors and friends from the farm communities over the county greeted each other and lingered to visit. Often the greeting was "Christmas Gift," and this meant whoever you said it to first, or before he said it to you, had to give you a gift. Gifts seldom changed hands and if so it would be a joke gift, but it was a custom grown folk seemed to have a lot of fun with, for they would laugh and point a finger at the victim and say, "Hah, I got you first!" While grown-ups were shouting "Christmas Gift" and visiting and shopping, the children were busy identifying each other in their unfamiliar Sunday clothes and acting uncommonly silly just from the novelty of gathering in town on a day other than Saturday. The older boys and girls met at Warren's Drug Store or around someone's family car, flirting and slyly pairing off.

Fireworks were part of the Christmas celebration, the one tradition that placed me in a state of panic so that I spent the day cowering beside Auntie lest a firecracker go off under my feet. I also dreaded stepping on the popping sand. Popping sand was a granular, grayish powder which when stepped on sent out sparks and a loud crackling noise. Boys loved it. They dashed about the street all day lighting firecrackers and spreading popping sand on the sidewalks, laughing and hooting and generally making a nuisance of themselves. At night, we were told, Roman candles were shot off from one of the vacant lots but we country kids never saw this spectacle because farmers had to get home before dark to attend to chores and animals. All in all, it was one of the most satisfactory days of the year and a perfect prelude to Christmas Day.

It was only on years when crops were poor or failed altogether because of some unfortunate circumstance that there was any grimness to the day. On those Christmas Eves the rocking horses and dolls and toy guns were left sitting in Greenfield's basement and the calls "Christmas Gift" were a little less cheerful. The tables would not be as abundant with cakes and pies and candies. More than likely the ambrosia would be missing as would fresh coconut and marshmallows on the candied sweet potatoes.

There would likely be no gift exchange at the school Christmas tree. This would be decided by a meeting of the teachers, seriously discussing whether some students, where there were several in a family, would be able to participate in a gift exchange. Gifts or no gifts, we survived very well singing carols and feasting our eyes on the tree.

The hard candy that Santa threw from his pack was more appreciated than other years.

There was no whining or pouting or long faces on Christmas morning on those years. Farm parents had a way of preparing even the smallest child for the inconsistencies of life on a West Texas dry-land farm. Early on we learned to watch for signs that told us unfailingly what kind of harvest to expect and we adjusted our dreams and desires to comply. Families would gather as usual to feast on whatever they could provide and to share the warmth of love and fellowship. The spirit of Christmas was in no way diminished just because the cotton crop had been meager.

We dreaded the eight-mile trip home from town on Christmas Eve because we knew it would be a cold ride. The standard heating system on all Model-T Fords (and other cars of that era) was two or three quilts stacked on the back seat. These were for placing across one's lap and wrapping up one's feet and legs but did not assure a comfortable ride. They merely served to keep one from turning blue and growing numb between home and destination. If you had not done so before, when the Model-T topped the Caprock and met the wind head-on, you quickly reached for the quilts. My warmest rides were when Auntie sat on one side of me and Aunt Mattie on the other on the back seat, the quilt spread over us and me snuggled down between them. That was coziness at its best. This was when we went visiting or to church; coming home from town I usually sat alone, pulled the quilt up to my chin and tucked my feet up under me, hoping to create a warm space. No sooner had I accomplished this than Uncle would slow the car down to turn into our driveway, which meant I had to get out to open the gate. Cold cruel world!

Uncle went straight to the front room, even before changing out of his town clothes, to make a fire in the heating stove and Auntie lit all the burners on the kerosene cookstove so the two rooms could warm up while we did the outside chores.

After the chores were done and the animals secured for the night, we sat in comfortable warmth at the kitchen table eating our hot cornmeal mush, rivulets of butter and cream mingling with the sugar we'd heaped onto it. All around the kitchen were pungent reminders of the excitement awaiting us on the following day. The pies, just visible on top of the cabinet, sat like impatient tempters waiting to be cut and eaten and exclaimed over. The fat, plump hen, her neck having been wrung the day before, her feathers plucked and singed and insides removed, sat inside the window cooler with a cloth respectfully covering her. Corn bread and biscuits were crumbled together, ready to be mixed into the dressing first thing in the morning. Packages and boxes of store-bought goodies were pushed into the pantry. The oranges and brown coconuts, in a basket on the sink stand, would be transformed into Auntie's delicious ambrosia.

There was no lingering around on Christmas Eve. I was eager to hang my black ribbed stocking and get into bed so Santa Claus could come.

There were few, if any, fireplaces in houses on the plains. Even before the land was cleared for farming there were only dried buffalo chips for burning. The houses that were built for the settlers had chimneys to accommodate heating stoves which burned coal. We West Texas kids hung our stockings on the back of a chair or the bed post or laid them on a chair seat by the heating stove. There was no less excitement than if it had been "hung by the chimney with care."

Winter turned the barren, flat, wind-weary landscape into a dirty, dull, unending brown vista and even on Christmas there was nothing to relieve the monotony. It was up to us to generate from within the glitter and glamour, the color and feel of the holiday for there was nothing from without to support or enhance the season — except when it snowed on Christmas Eve. Usually it was only a light powdering of snow; nevertheless, on these occasions we felt we had been especially blessed. The snow gave a special dimension to the celebration. It was much easier to expect Santa Claus and to visualize the Baby Jesus in a manger when there was a covering of snow turning our plains into a strange and mysterious land. With snowflakes whirling past the bedroom window we could snuggle down in bed beneath layers of quilts, nightcaps covering our ears and drift and dream until sleep overtook us, knowing our bleak, brown world would be completely changed when we woke up.

I remember the last Christmas before I had to accept the awful truth about Santa Claus. At first light of day I was out of bed. Oblivious to the shock of the cold floor on my feet, I skimmed across the room and flung open the door to the front room. There was my stocking, just where I had hung it, bulging with goodies, and sitting on the chair was the most beautiful doll I had ever seen. Long brown curls of real hair framed her lovely china face, her bright blue eyes were fringed with lashes and she was dressed in a delicate blue taffeta dress with white stockings and little black slippers on her feet. I picked her up and to my astonishment her eyes closed; I held her up straight and her eyes opened. I was speechless; this special, beautiful doll was really mine. It was as if I were caught up in a wonderful dream. "Her name is Dorothy," I announced without hesitation. Dorothy was the only suitable name for anything so lovely.

On the floor beside Dorothy was a little white chest that Uncle had built. The lid had brass hinges and a clasp that fastened with a key. In the chest were dainty garments for Dorothy which Auntie had painstakingly fashioned — a red wool coat with cap to match, a pink print dress with tiny buttons and lace, a flannel nightgown and nightcap and, folded in the bottom of the chest, a hand-pieced quilt just the right size to cover her.

And there was still more! My stocking was waiting to be emptied. It was stretched beyond recognition for a huge orange was stuffed into the very top. It was only with Uncle's help it came popping out, followed by a rainbow of hard candy which rolled out into my eager hands.

One of the best parts of growing up during those years was that most of the treats were seasonal. Hard candy was seldom available except at Christmas which made it especially desirable. There were clear red berry-shaped pieces, circular pieces with infinitesimally small flowers in the center which did not disappear as you let it melt in your mouth but was there as long as a sliver was left, tart lemon drops that were sugary on the outside, grape-flavored balls, twisted green and yellow ribbons of taffy, red peppermint sticks. Examining each piece and making a selection of which to eat and which to hold back for later was not a decision to take lightly, but this careful consideration only served to intensify the deliciousness.

In the middle of the stocking, and even harder to get out, was the biggest apple I'd ever seen, then came the nuts — almonds, walnuts, Brazil nuts and pecans — and in the toe was a very special treat, a fresh coconut. Reaching down into the stocking I could feel its coarse, hairy shell. And as I fondled it, reluctant to bring it out, a sense of nostalgia swept over me, a knowing deep inside that Christmas would never again be the same and that I would remember this one long after the others had faded away into the dust of time.

Long before the noon hour family folk would begin to arrive. Grandma, Grandpa, and Aunt Mattie with Uncle Bob and Aunt Rosa, having arrived the night before, would drive over from Grandpa's farm two miles away. Soon other aunts, uncles and cousins would be coming up the front walk, carrying covered dishes and baskets of food, the cousins racing to the front door. All at once, the house was running over with folk, greeting each other, laughing, cousins chattering as each one tried to be first to tell what Santa had left for them. The girls brought their dolls or tea sets or something from their gifts; the boys displayed new balls, knives, toy guns and puzzles made from metal rings. Finally, to bring order to the day, we were sent to one of the bedrooms to play.

Dinner was a feast. We ate in shifts: at "first table" the men and Grandma were served, then the aunts and other adults and last the children. This was accepted order for all family meals, no matter where or when, whenever there was an overflow of guests to be seated. The children always had plenty of everything and never considered any other arrangement. In fact, we would have been embarrassed to eat before our elders had been served, and it was certainly more fun than eating with them. It was not hard to wait until "last table" for throughout the morning aunts had been handing out snacks. All any child had to do was show up in the kitchen and say, "I'm hungry," and he was handed a tasty tidbit.

This was one meal we could eat whatever we wanted, in any amount. If we were willing to risk a stomachache we could make our meal of pie and cake. I would gladly have made mine from the ambrosia — resplendent in a footed glass bowl, its orange slices and flaked coconut delicately dressed with a thin sauce Auntie had made. Aunt Mattie's chocolate cake, sitting in its accustomed place, had undergone a change by the time our turn came, but there was still plenty for us. We left the table with stomachs overstuffed, yet with an eye on the leftover goodies for later in the day.

All good things must eventually end; the day began to draw to a close. Play-weary cousins were rounded up, the older cousins helping the younger ones locate toys and caps and coats. Aunts and uncles bundled them into the cars as they called their last goodbyes, waving their arms from the car windows as they drove away. Suddenly the house was very quiet. Another Christmas had come and gone. The orange-colored glow of the setting sun held a touch of nostalgia; it had been a good day, a satisfying day, but there was a reluctance to release it and let it become another memory.

> I heard a bird sing in the dark of December,
> A magical thing; sweet to remember.
> We are nearer to May than we were in September.
> — Oliver Hereford

But May was far from our thoughts. The best of winter was yet to come — plenty of time to read and dream through the long, dark nights, snow ice cream after the first snowfall, the cozy excitement of being isolated by a first-rate blizzard, and those wonderful do-nothing days that lay like an oasis between Christmas Day and New Year's Day.

The week between Christmas and New Year's Day was a special time for farm folk in our community, a laid-back time when the only work we did was the routine morning and evening chores that must be performed for the sake of the animals. We spent these days sitting around the heating stove doing nothing, daydreaming, dozing, the women folk doing handwork, maybe.

We ate leftover Christmas goodies, so about all the cooking Auntie (or any of the womenfolk) did was breakfast — the same every morning all year long — biscuits, big, soft, fluffy southern biscuits, sausage or bacon homemade from our own hogs, and fried eggs. Sitting on a tray in the middle of our round oak kitchen table were peach and cherry preserves, wild plum jelly, apple jelly — fruits of Auntie and Aunt Mattie's summer labors. There was plenty of butter, churned from thick cream right in this same kitchen where we were at that moment watching its melted goodness drip out the sides of our hot biscuit. A big pitcher of cream and a full sugar bowl were nearby for "doctoring up the coffee," as Uncle would say. No one had ever heard of drinking black coffee. Had anyone asked for coffee in such a denuded state they would have been looked upon with curiosity, if not suspicion.

Uncle made no effort to do extra outside chores during this week — those could wait until later. Auntie, likewise, did only what was necessary; washing and ironing could wait and no projects were undertaken. Not even much visiting went on between friends and relatives. It was a quiet, reflective time, a time to do anything or nothing.

Children had the whole week to play with new Christmas toys. If we grew tired of playing then we could sit by the window, look into space and wonder what the world was like beyond the horizon, or daydream about what we would be when we grew up. Or curl up with a good book. In those years it was not considered necessary that children be constantly entertained or active in some type of group activity. Nor was there the distraction of television nor even radio to listen to. The '20s left plenty of time to a child's own discretion, to mull over questions and figure out answers. Our imaginations were completely unstructured, so we enjoyed the best of all childhood games, pretending and projecting oneself into the picture. Even with disturbances going on around and about us, our own personal world was bound about with security. We were allowed to experience childhood.

During those years any recreational activity was entirely dependent upon our imagination and creativity. We devised and made many of our toys and games. Boys fashioned miniature carts and wagons from pieces of wire and tin or other tidbits they found lying unused around the farmyard. A wooden apple crate together with wheels salvaged from worn-out farm equipment made a dandy racing car. Slingshot stocks were whittled with a jackknife from a board picked off the scrap lumber pile and from a car inner tube, worn beyond repairing; lengths of rubber bands were cut and affixed to the stock handles, a piece of leather from a worn-out glove to cradle the stone, and a boy had a great toy. He could hold target practice on anything from a bird to a fence post. Or the old barnyard rooster or the family dog would do if no one was watching and a brother or cousin didn't tattle on him. In West Texas finding a rock or stone was the hard part. The older boys saddled their horses and rode around the community in groups, gathering at each other's houses. Boys played endless games of marbles and catch and shinney. It was better than summer for there was no dread of field work hanging over them.

A row of chairs set in a line became a train. My dolls and I took many trips this way. There is no limit to where one can go on such a train. The neatest kind of playhouse could be made by draping a quilt over a couple of dining chairs. Old mail-order catalogs and magazines furnished an unlimited supply of paper dolls, and a cardboard box could easily be converted into a dollhouse.

If weather permitted, we might get together with neighbor kids to play games or kinfolk might drop over one afternoon with a gaggle of cousins to break the peace and quiet. Regardless of how much or how little activity went on during this interim between Christmas and New Year's Day, we were allowed to be as lazy as we wanted to be. We could "sleep in" — a very rare treat for a farm child since we all had our assigned chores and were expected to help at any time a farm job needed a hand. This made lying in bed a luxury and privilege connected with this special week.

We could eat candy, cake or pie at our own discretion. This is why a well-stuffed stocking on Christmas morning was a cherished gift, carefully scrutinized for the number of its contents. If we were careful to count pieces and divide by the number of days, we knew how many pieces of hard candy, how many nuts and how much fruit we could allow ourselves per day and have our supply last through New Year's Day. There were no restrictions on how many times a day one could reach a hand inside the lard bucket for divinity, Mexican orange or date loaf candy. It was there to be eaten until it was all gone. The same was true of pie and cake. The only food prepared especially for this week was baked ham. We sliced it, fried it, made sandwiches and ate it plain. Sometime Auntie would bestir herself and boil the bones and leavings from the Christmas baked hen and make a pot of tender, chewy dumplings. We popped lots of corn. We kids made popcorn balls — a sticky, messy job, but fun to eat.

It was a good time to get out the photograph album — Auntie had time to tell me who all the starched-up, unsmiling kinfolk were in the yellowed pictures and tintypes. It was fun for her, too. Auntie had a memory box and Aunt Mattie had a whole trunk full of memories. They allowed me to take out and hold and handle these treasures. In Aunt Mattie's trunk was a red calico vest that had belonged to Aunt Ida, twin to Aunt Ada, who I never knew for she died of malaria fever when she was twelve years old. It made me sad to see it. There were trinkets and keepsakes and letters tied with faded ribbons and a stack of postcards. Some of the cards had been delivered on the rural route without ever going through a post office. The mail carrier had canceled the one-cent stamp with an indelible pencil and dropped it in the proper box along his route.

Some of the cards had humorous pictures, some had local scenes of courthouses, schoolhouses, hotels or main streets with buggies and horses, and some had elaborate flowers or beautiful women posed with wistful looks and high fancy hairdos. All of them had messages which I felt free to read, reasoning that the mail carrier had done so. "Dear Miss Mattie: Will you be attending the singing at

Rising Star next Sunday afternoon? May I sit with you? Devotedly, Winthrop P. Cooksy," was a typical message. I would read and wonder if Aunt Mattie sat with Winthrop P. Cooksy and if he was handsome and if he thought Aunt Mattie pretty. Then one would read, "Hah — saw you last Saturday with You-Know-Who," and signed "Guess Who." That would set my imagination working. Who was You-Know-Who and what were he and Aunt Mattie doing last Saturday? And who was Guess Who? No matter how many times I read them I was entertained.

This was a good time for Auntie to take out the box of quilt scraps and have a look at possibilities for making a pretty quilt. Patterns were pored over and their merits considered. Uncle got out the whetstone and sharpened his pocketknives — the pearl-handled one he carried when he dressed up and the Barlow he carried in his overalls for use around the farm. He'd ask Auntie if her kitchen knives needed sharpening. Such little chores relieved any tendency to boredom. Mostly, Uncle enjoyed the luxury of just sitting, mixed equally with dozing and reading. These were good days; rare and coveted.

On the back part of a baked hen there is a little portion of meat no bigger than one's thumb that is neither white nor dark but is a succulent morsel hidden in a small concave section just above the rib cage where the shoulder would be, if a hen had a shoulder. This delicacy, enough for only a few good bites, is called the tenderloin of the hen. It is the best way to describe those days between Christmas and New Year's Day — they were the "tenderloin" of the year.

January was sure to bring weather; hopefully, it would be snow. The farmers wanted it so there would be moisture for spring planting; for us kids it meant eating hand-fuls as we frolicked through it, snowball fights, high drifts to fall into and no school.

The first snow of winter brought a stir of excitement. Blowing straight out of the north, across the flat plains, it developed while we slept, greeting us in the early morning light with a considerable drop in temperature and steel-gray clouds, like a snug toboggan cap, covering the sky. Waking on a morning to this kind of weather aroused an uncontrollable stirring somewhere deep inside, an intoxi-cating anticipation, a rapture that made one want to shout, jump up and down or do something out of the ordinary.

It developed quickly. Looking through the north kitchen window, we saw signs all around — a sharp gust of wind caught at Uncle's mackinaw causing him to reach out and draw it more closely about him as he made his way across the barnyard. A few feathery flakes dropped here and there. A sudden push of wind stirred the barren limbs of the mulberry tree. Then a flurry of white swept across the yard as the storm tested its strength, the wind muttering around the corner of the house and rattling a window. The preliminaries over, the storm settled down to a steady fall of snow. The barn and chicken house and outbuildings were seen through a gauzy curtain and all neighboring farms were quickly out of sight. No cars nor buggies nor horseback riders would pass by on the road today. Nor was there any use to watch for the mail carrier for he would not get over his route. We were locked into silent white seclusion.

Snow was never a "blanket of snow"; a blanket was something that kept you warm in bed at night after the snow fell. Snow was snow, transforming the garden fence into a wall and building a hill in the backyard; it remodeled the chicken house into a strange, enchanted cottage; it piled against the back door, closing out the rest of the world, making the house a fortress with Auntie, Uncle and me cozy in its protecting warmth.

There would be no school that day. There were no radios nor television to switch on and listen for an announcement; it was simply understood that on any day it snowed there would be no school. If the sun shone the following day we could expect school, as usual; if the sky was still dark and threatening, we stayed home another day.

On any other morning breakfast was the first order of the day, but when a snowstorm was imminent the chores were attended to first and breakfast came second. So first thing Auntie did after coming back inside from helping Uncle with the milking was break the ice on the bucket of water sitting on the kitchen sink — it had been drawn the night before — so she could set the coffee to percolating. The aroma as it perked merrily on the stove gave a warmth to the room and added a special facet to this out-of-the-ordinary day.

After breakfast dishes were washed, dried and put away on the cabinet shelf, there was nothing to do except contemplate the fun of an uninterrupted day of reading, playing, watching through the window as the white flakes chased each other down the sky, and looking forward expectantly to the time when Auntie would agree that the drifts were plenty deep enough to get clean, unblemished snow for the ice cream.

One of the bonuses of a good deep snowfall was this very special treat — snow ice cream. Auntie, bundled up in her cap, coat and boots and armed with her biggest pan, would dash outside to the highest drift and scoop up a panful. Back inside the house she worked quickly to put the delectable dish together. Sugar, cream and vanilla flavoring were mixed and then ever so carefully folded into the snow so that it kept its fluffy texture but was thoroughly blended with the ingredients. A delightful dish. A little later on in the day we could count on that same big pan heaped with popcorn. Popcorn and snow ice cream — what a treat on a cold, snowy winter day.

Late in the afternoon the snow stopped falling and the wind died down. Uncle, restless from being inside all day yet reluctant to leave the comfort of the house, put on his mackinaw and his cap with the ear flaps, pulled on his boots and pushed open the back door, letting in an icy gust of cold air. He stepped out into the boot-high accumulation and, leaving a jagged trail behind him, made his way to the barns. The only one who really wanted to go outdoors was me. I could hardly wait to wade into the drifts, getting snow down my boot tops and on my clothes, and eat handfuls of it, feeling its gauziness melt on my tongue. Kids ate lots of snow back then and to my knowledge no one suffered any bad consequences. Of course, there was not the pollution to worry with then as there is now.

How strange and beautiful the farm looked in the steely late afternoon light. The haystacks were topped with a white fluffy icing and as Uncle pulled out the bundles to feed the mules and cows, it showered down on him. He'd pitch the bundles over the corral-type fence and the mules, confined all day to the boredom of their shelter and hungry, would race out, pushing and nipping each other to be first to get to the feed. Soon they would have the sparkling ground in the barnyard trampled and dirty. After the cows were fastened into their stanchions and fed their usual provisions and milked, they would be thrown feed bundles, too.

With satisfaction Uncle looked out across his plowed field and saw the furrows level with snow. This was good. There would be moisture for spring planting. He would sleep well that night and so would I, for when I went to bed, Auntie would tuck a warm flatiron, wrapped in a towel, to my feet and before it lost its heat I would be asleep.

Next morning the sun would be shining, making a million diamonds as it reflected across the snow. This meant school would be in session. I dreaded going, for the boys would be there early, lined up with an arsenal of snowballs ready to pelt everyone who entered the school grounds. The thing to do was run fast, dodging as many as possible. Recesses were miserable. A boy would sneak up behind a girl and if she was not holding her coat collar tightly around her neck, he would grab the collar open and cram snow down her back. How we girls hated it! Boys rolled one another in the drifts and chose up sides for snowball fights. There was lots of shouting and screaming and giggling and by the time the bell rang to go inside, everyone who had not received permission to stay inside the building trudged in tired, cold and smelling of wet wool and rubber overshoes. As clothes warmed and began to dry, the worse they smelled until the fumes were almost unbearable.

Mr. Robinson, in his wisdom, often cut short the noon recess and canceled last recess and by so doing no doubt avoided a lot of absentees due to colds and flu. At any rate, by the time school was out that afternoon kids were tired of the game and dreading the cold walk home.

Winter was not all Thanksgiving, Christmas and snowy days. There were plenty of dull, cold days that seemed endless. At school, when we were sent outside for recess, it was too cold and windy to enjoy playing games so we hovered on the south side of the building in the weak winter sunshine, waiting for the bell to ring so we could line up and march back inside. The walk home loomed before us like a death march. Evening chores were a dreaded inevitability, but cows had to be fed and milked, hogs and mules had to be fed, eggs gathered and grain spread for hens and roosters — these chores had to be done whether or not we felt like bundling up and facing the weather.

The sun dropped beneath the horizon at an early hour so the evenings were long and sometimes boringly tedious. Lamp light was a poor substitute for daylight. We had two kerosene lamps and an Aladdin lamp. The Aladdin lamp burned kerosene, too, but had a fragile white cone-shaped wick that put out a steady white light, much more desirable than the yellow, flickering light of the regular lamps. We lit all three of them as soon as it was dark.

Uncle, who liked to read, leaned back in his chair beside the square oak table which sat against the west wall between two doors that led into the bedrooms and on which the two regular lamps stood. Auntie sat on the opposite side of the table to do embroidery work or piece on a quilt or read. I sat at the library table in the middle of the room, my back to the heating stove and my nose in a book.

Books were my passion. I read anything that had a back and printed pages. Finding something to read was the problem. There was no public library in Post, our county seat. The one at Ragtown school consisted of six five-foot shelves in the northeast corner of Mr. Robinson's class-room. On these shelves was a set of Books of Knowledge which were well worn from constant use and a set of encyclopedias, equally well used; *Webster's Unabridged Dictionary* and various volumes of literature, including all the works of Shakespeare; English poets and writers, American authors and a small collection of supplementary books for subjects taught in the classrooms. Not a very imposing library but equal to, if not superior in some cases, to all the country schools in Garza County. I was luckier than most of my classmates because my Aunt Corra, who lived in Post, owned a small collection of books which she generously allowed me to borrow — as often and as many as I cared to take home with me. Many of them were read over and over again. And most of us owned a few books and would trade them back and forth between classmates.

Some evenings Auntie and Uncle played games with me. All three of us liked a good rousing game of Pollyanna, a board game no longer available except possibly in a junk shop or antique store. I spent hours playing endless games of Solitary and playing jacks against an imaginary opponent. Of course, there was homework to do. Auntie required that all homework be finished and checked by her before any fun and games.

While I was in school all day Uncle and Auntie were busy doing farm and household projects they did not have time for in the busy months of the year. It was the time for making additions and repairs in the house, redecorating. One winter Uncle built Auntie a quilt box. This was a necessary and desirable piece of furniture. Some households had elaborate ones. Aunt Clara had a huge one made of dark carved wood and cedar-lined. Mrs. Henderson had one that had strange Oriental designs on the lid. Uncle designed Auntie's from a walnut bed that had been stored for years in Grandpa's barn. The tall ornate headboard was used for the back and the shorter footboard was the front. The lid and sides were made from new material and stained to match the back and front. It made a very attractive piece of furniture. When the lid was closed Auntie spread one of her pretty embroidered dresser scarves across it and set a blue vase and a bisque doll on top. The doll had been a gift from her first boyfriend when she was thirteen years old. The quilt box sat on the south wall in my bedroom. After awhile it became a favorite storage chest not only for beautiful, colorful quilts, but for special items such as cards and letters Auntie wanted to keep, head scarves too nice to wear, an intimidating package of legal looking papers I was told never to touch, and an old purse Auntie kept her butter and egg money in, letting it accumulate for buying special things. Our first piece of elegant furniture, a divan upholstered in cut velvet, was purchased from this fund.

If any room needed new wallpaper — and invariably there was one that did — the new paper was put up during these winter months. This undertaking could be closely compared to setting up the heating stove. I was usually in school, and glad of it, when papering was done.

It was important to choose a calm, mild day, the wind in abeyance and no clouds in sight. I cannot explain the rationale for this but it apparently was important, for at breakfast Auntie would say, "Looks like a nice day. We had better get the back room papered today." Uncle would agree with noticeable lack of enthusiasm. "While you take Helen Maude to school I'll put sheets over the furniture and start tearing off the paper."

That was the first step — tear the existing paper from the wall, pull down the canvas (a thin cotton net fabric used as a backing for the paper), which was put up with tacks, and pull the tacks out of the wall. This first step alone was sufficient provocation to bring one's patience to the breaking point. Every time a section of paper was pulled down a shower of dust, dried paste and scraps of paper fell with it. Then the whole mess had to be cleaned up before the new paper job could commence. Next the new canvas was stretched upon the wall and tacked into place. It had to fit like a kid glove; there must not be a single wrinkle in it because the paper would be pasted directly on top of it. Now came the intricate cutting so the pattern matched at the seams — this was of utmost importance. It was understandable that by this time tempers had warmed considerably. Many remarks began with "Mr. Mangum" and "Madam" while the walls were transformed into a flower garden or stripes were carefully hung straight up and down. Returning home from school I received, instead of the usual cheerful greeting, an admonition: "Don't slam the door! And don't go back there to look because I want that door to stay closed until the paste dries." To have newly hung paper crack was a tragedy too terrible to consider and, apparently, a change in temperature or a slammed door could cause that to happen. The smell of new wallpaper permeated the house, giving it an unfamiliarity that was both stimulating and satisfying.

The bright spot in winter was Valentine's Day. Once again the construction paper made an appearance on our school desks. We were set to making red and white hearts, and roses and weaving baskets from alternate strips of red and white. The window panes were decorated, this time with hearts, and hearts were strung on a cord and hung above the blackboard. We covered a large cardboard box with colorful crepe paper and decorated it with paper hearts and flowers and ruffles of crepe paper. A slit was cut in the lid for dropping in the valentines. It set on a corner of the teacher's desk so that every time we looked up we could admire our work of art. We used up our tablets making valentines, coloring and decorating them; most of them ended up in the waste basket. All of mine did.

In the '20s valentines were beautiful and expressed nice sentiments — sentimental verses about love and friendship, wishing wishes of joy and happiness, coy references to courtship and devotion. There were some comic ones but these were never exchanged at school. The cards were festooned with garlands and lacy borders, cupids, angels, all in pretty colors of pink, lavender, or red. Some were constructed so they unfolded to stand up; these were reserved for someone special.

An honor coveted above all others was to be a valentine "postman." On Valentine's Day two students were chosen by the teacher to assist her as "postmen" to deliver the cards to the recipients' desks. I longed to be selected but, alas, the honor was never mine. We'd watch as the stack grew taller and taller on some desks and on others only a few were delivered, all the time keeping careful count of our own collection.

Juanita was a fat little girl who we all poked fun at. She took our unmerciful teasing and taunting in stride and on Valentine's Day she got even with us — she gave every classmate a nice store-bought card. This made us ashamed and for a week afterwards we were nice to her. She was an intelligent girl, always clean, as were her four brothers, and bore with dignity and serenity the barbs and jibes her classmates so unkindly inflicted upon her. I would have caught it at home if word had ever come to my parents that I took part in such nefarious acts. But I was guilty, wanting to identify with the "in" group, and afterwards ashamed, wanting to tell Juanita so but not knowing how to go about doing it.

After school let out we were full of chatter about the number we received and from whom. This interesting subject carried over to the next day for we brought our valentines to school to compare and gloat over at recess.

Valentine's Day made us yearn for spring. Often, about this time, there was a lull in the weather. The temperature climbed and the wind died down, giving us a foretaste of spring and raising hope that the worst of winter was over. It was in this kind of attitude we were most certain to have a real, for-sure-enough West Texas blizzard.

There being very little between the West Texas plains and the Canadian border (where allegedly all our "weather" came from) to slow or stop it, the wind and snow could have a heyday, freezing cattle that got caught out away from shelter, breaking down fences, blowing farm buildings over. Once our two-hole privy was laid flat on the ground and buried under a mountain of snow — a tragic inconvenience!

I never understood how grown-ups instinctively knew it was a blizzard on the way and not an ordinary norther. Something in the way the atmosphere felt would tell them, or perhaps they observed the cattle grow nervous with a keen desire to get to shelter. If we were at school when a blizzard started moving in there was a big scramble to get all students on their way home as quickly as possible. Teachers and older students anxiously helped little ones get scarves tied, caps on, overshoes buckled and into the right coat. Don't stop along the way, run, hurry!

This was one of those rare times when some of the other fathers came to get their children in the family car.

By noon the sky would be a solid cloud, the atmosphere dark and brooding; by mid-afternoon a sharp, steady wind was blowing from the north, accompanied by spasmodic flurries of snow. An extra supply of coal and kindling had been brought inside the house, the cookstove and lamps filled with kerosene, quilts hung across the north and west windows, animals comfortably stabled, dogs and cats in their accustomed places, and families safe inside waiting for the ominous lull that signaled the arrival of the blizzard. The lull was a hush, a silence so deep that it was a relief when the storm struck — a gale of wind so terrific, so forceful that the house shook on its foundations. Gusting down the chimney it sent ashes swirling from the stove grate into the room. Then the blinding snow. Looking out the window all we could see was an avalanche of snow too dense to see through, accompanied by the sad and eerie sound of the shrieking, moaning wind. There was no knowing how long the blizzard would last, through the night or several days.

Regardless of whether it was of short or long duration, the blizzard stopped as abruptly as it began. One would walk to the window to look out and see an impenetrable wall of snow, turn back to the stove to get warm and suddenly the wind had stopped its howling, the snow had thinned to a feathering of flakes and a faint, weak sun was making an effort to shine through.

Understandably, there was a cautious return to normal activity. The dog was first, putting his nose out of the mules' shelter where he had been holed up for the duration and cautiously feeling his way outside. The cats ventured out of the cow shed. But the mules and cows were content to remain inside their comfortable shelters and watch Uncle as he walked about the place surveying the damage. A huge drift, taller than Uncle's six-foot height, lay against the cowpen fence. Part of the roofing on the barn was torn loose. The chicken house, hidden behind snow hills, was hard to find. A great mountain of snow must be moved from the corncrib door; the coal bin was out of sight. Yet, in contrast, there were many bare spaces over the yards and field where the wind had swept it clean. There was a mystical aura, a sense of strange adventure about a blizzard.

One of my most memorable of all blizzards was once when Odie Roberts came home with me from school to spend the night. To our delight, a blizzard blew in and lasted for two days. If there had been telephone service such as we have today, Odie's grandma would have called the school and left a message that she was to come home. A telephone in a country school was unheard of in the '20s, and, in fact, very few farm families had one. In some cases this was an advantage, and this was such a case.

Arrangements to stay overnight with a friend were made over a period of several days via notes dispatched from parent to parent through the two friends who were negotiating the "stay all night." Since Odie lived with her grandparents and I with my aunt and uncle, we found a special bond from our first day in school. We were best friends and spent nights together as often as we could arrange it. She lived four miles northeast of school and I lived two and half miles southwest of school, so we had little chance to play except at school and when we could arrange an overnight at one of our houses.

On Monday, after getting Auntie's consent, I sent a note home by Odie: "Dear Mrs. Roberts: Will you please let Odie spend Thursday night with me? Its alright with Auntie. Helen Maude." Next morning (Tuesday) Odie brought a note from Mrs. Roberts for Auntie saying Odie could stay all night on Thursday if she was sure it was alright. Back would go a note to Mrs. Roberts: "We are expecting Odie to spend Thursday night with us. Mrs. Mangum." By then it was Wednesday. So Thursday Odie came to school carrying her nightgown, clean black sateen bloomers, black ribbed stockings, and other necessities in a little carpetbag which she stowed under her desk. It's understandable, after these elaborate and tedious arrangements, that even if the sky was falling, Odie was not going to do otherwise than get into the back seat of our Model-T and go home with me, just as her grandmother had given her permission to do. So even though the weather looked threatening and the wind had picked up, when school was out we progressed as planned. Probably Uncle had a premonition the weather was going into one of its tantrums but he said nothing, so we went happily, giggling and talking in the back seat, planning what we would do first thing when we got to my house.

We were ready to climb into bed when the storm struck. Huddling under the covers, Odie wearing one of my nightcaps, we lay listening and talking and sharing secrets as the storm raged around the corners of the house, snug with quilts covering my bedroom windows, secure in our comfort and safety.

The surprise came next morning when we expected to awaken to a blue sky and bright sunshine glittering on the ice and snow but instead the room was gloomy and we could hear the wind blowing. Above the noise we heard Auntie and Uncle talking so I popped out of bed and peeked through the door into the front room where they were sitting by the stove.

"Is it time to get up?"

Auntie laughed. "Guess what time it is."

"I don't know — eight o'clock?"

"Nine-thirty."

"Oh, we've missed school!"

"No school today," Uncle said.

I pushed through the door and to the window and saw the blizzard was still going full force. Uncle and Auntie went to the kitchen so Odie and I could dress in the warm front room while Auntie stirred up batter for fat, puffy buttermilk pancakes for us. This special treatment — sleeping late and having breakfast just the two of us — was a glorious way to start our surprise "holiday" together. So we gave ourselves over to hours of playing, reading aloud to each other, inventing games and playing Pollyanna with Auntie and Uncle. There were pans of popcorn to munch on and we helped Auntie make a batch of divinity candy which we had to eat with a spoon for it didn't set up.

Sometime during Friday night the wind ceased its blowing and the snow stopped falling so that we awoke next morning to a fine day: the sky an inverted china-blue bowl and brilliant sun competing with the blinding white snow. It was that afternoon before Uncle could get the car started and take Odie home. We reluctantly said goodbye, wanting to prolong this red-letter experience, one we would remember and talk about and relive and discuss around our friends — embellishing it and making it appear it was something we had planned ourselves.

Winter was a good time in the '20s on a farm in West Texas.

THE DARK OF
THE MOON

There were events in our life which had no season of their own. They could happen at any season and did, unpredictable and unwelcome, whether it was in the midst of spring planting or in the dark days of winter. Those inevitable circumstances of life that sprang out at us and held us immobile for a space of time — bitter, black-bread experiences — were life-altering hesitations in our daily, seasonal existence. Sickness, death, fire (burn-out), farm accidents, and loss of farm animals were among the list of our personal sadnesses. Then, as now, there was no convenient time for the tragedies and worries, hard times and heartaches that life handed us. We dealt with these tragedies within the scope of the lifestyle of that era.

Sickness was a sinister cloud, likely to cut out the sunshine at any time, irrespective of circumstances or the time of year. A farmer could be laid up in his sickbed in the middle of the planting season or the frenzy of harvesting the cotton crop. A wife or child might be desperately ill and need undivided, careful attention in the height of the summer canning season. It could be in the coldest part of winter when the sickbed was moved into the front room where the heating stove was kept going night and day to keep the patient comfortable. Sickness was no respecter of time or person.

Ours could be said to be a remarkably healthy family, holding Grandpa up as an exemplary specimen of what sensible living on the clean, sun-cured, wide-open spaces of West Texas could produce. For breakfast Grandpa buttered three of Aunt Mattie's good biscuits. With two of them he ate two fried eggs, a piece or two of home-cured bacon or sausage; the third biscuit he covered with thick, black sorghum syrup. He ate with relish and appreciation what, in his opinion, was the perfect meal to start a day. After he left the table, he set his black Planters hat on his head and went out to walk his field. This was a necessary walk so that he could see how the crop was growing, whether it was time to get hoe hands to clear out the weeds, what plowing was necessary and in the fall, during harvest, to see if the cotton stalks were being picked clean of bolls, whether the feed was ready for Mr. Morris to bring over his binder. By now he was retired from active farming but it was necessary to make a daily check for he was his own farm manager — as any good farmer should be.

He walked the half mile to the back of the field, across the half section, down and across again to make a perfect square back to the house. He only missed taking this walk if it should rain — a rare occasion in West Texas — or if there was a raging blizzard in the dark of winter. I attribute his lean body and good health to these daily walks and to his stock of patent medicines.

He had a dozen or so bottles of various sizes, shapes and colors set in a line across the back of an oak dresser that sat in the front room. In the morning he carefully surveyed his stockpile, selected one of the bottles, un-corked it, lifted it to his lips and took a swig, making an awful grimace and sputtering mightily at the taste. At night he repeated the treatment before going to bed. The names of the patent medicines are unknown to me, but I now wonder, since he was a teetotaler, if he knew most of them contained eighteen percent alcohol. From the time I can remember to the day he died, at age ninety, he never varied from his routine except when he was away from home. His walking and his patent medicines were his for-mula for good health; it was as good as any formula seven-ty years ago because about the only treatment available at that time was chicken soup, "ease" medicine and prayer.

When someone in the community got sick, a neighbor or family member hooked up the buggy or saddled a horse or cranked up the Model-T and went to Ragtown to summon Dr. Tweet. By the time Dr. Tweet died tele-phones had been installed in some of the farm homes so that someone could ring up Central at Post and ask them to call Dr. Williams.

Anxiety gave way to hope and confidence when Dr. Williams stopped his car at the front gate, got out and walked onto the porch, carrying his black bag. About all the doctor could do was take the patient's temperature, ask where he hurt, put his stethoscope to his ears and listen to the body sounds, thump the chest a few times, look in the throat and at the tongue and in the ears. After this ritual, he opened his black bag and took from it several glass bottles containing powders. With a small, thin spatula he took small amounts of powder from first one and another of the bottles, then mixed and divided it into doses. These doses were placed on small squares of paper which were carefully folded and left in the care of a family member to administer as directed. "Now Mrs. Mangum," Dr. Williams would say, in his soft Alabama drawl, "give Mr. Mangum one of these in a glass of water any time he seems restless or feverish." Then he would tell her to keep Uncle out of drafts and to bathe his body with damp towels if his fever came up. Also, to place a folded wet cloth on the forehead and change it often to keep it cool. These were well-known treatments. When Dr. Williams left he told Auntie to call him if there was a turn for the worse through the night. Many times doctors, in those years, would get out of bed in the wee hours of the night to attend a patient.

Word quickly spread over the neighborhood when someone was sick. Soon concerned friends were knocking at the door asking if they were needed to sit up at night, or bearing a pot of freshly made chicken soup for the invalid, or offering to go to Mr. Parrish's store for lemons. Lemonade was as essential to recovery as chicken soup and ease medicine. There was always a glass of lemonade sitting on the table by the bed beside the folded squares the doctor had left. If the husband was the stricken one then the neighborhood men organized the nights each would take a turn sitting up. Likewise, if it was a wife or child, the womenfolk took turns. No one sick enough to need a doctor was allowed to lie alone, untended through a long, dark night. Someone was with them from sundown to sunup. A lamp was left burning in the sickroom at night. A card was placed behind one of the prongs that held the chimney — this shaded the patient's eyes from the light. Also, the men offered to help with any farm chores the wife or children could not handle. If the sickness lingered on they would bring their mules and plows and do whatever work was needed in the field. Crops were not allowed to suffer just because a man was too sick to plow or gather. I remember very well one summer when Uncle had pneumonia and a long convalescence. Early one bright morning we heard noise outside and looking out the window we saw farmer friends with their teams of mules pulling go-devils (a plow that cuts weeds from the beds between the rows of cotton) into our driveway. They kept coming until we counted six of them come to plow Uncle's crop. Uncle was on the road to recovery from that morning's work.

There was not much smiling or laughter around a farm home when there was a sick person in bed. Screen doors were closed quietly and we talked in soft tones. Neighbors, friends and relatives came and went, bringing their concern and anything they felt might make the patient more comfortable or tempt a flagging appetite — the lightest of custards, a bottle of grape juice or a nice piece of fruit.

Eventually, the glad hour would come when the hot, flushed face and burning forehead would begin to perspire — the fever had broken! This is what the concerned ones had been praying for. A great sigh of relief went up and the worried wife, mother or father smiled for the first time in days. The crisis was passed. One day soon the big rocking chair in the front room would be draped with a quilt and the invalid tenderly supported so his weakened legs would carry him to the chair. Pillows were arranged at his back and head and the quilt folded over his legs. The welcome news went out to friends and kinfolk that "he is able to sit up." This meant the nightly vigils could be stopped. Now only the long days of convalescence were to be endured until the patient was well again but this would be borne gladly and patiently. Once again loving hands, ease medicine and chicken soup had won the battle.

Home remedies were our fortress against the storms of life. Every household knew a score of remedies for most every eventuality and these were always administered with determination, confidence, and, when necessary, force.

If a child came home from school looking droopy and had a runny nose, his mother put him to bed that night after greasing his chest with Vicks salve, swabbing some up his nose and, to be on the safe side, forcing a big dollop down his throat. This treatment usually was sufficient. But if the cold persisted and he started to run a temperature and cough, then the mustard plaster was brought into service. When the top was unscrewed from the jar of mustard plaster the fumes brought tears to the eyes. This was only a mild foretaste of what was to follow. The chest was exposed and a coating of mustard applied. It began to burn the moment it touched the skin, but worse yet a hot flannel cloth was laid over it and the bed clothes were pulled up to further insulate the plaster. This treatment was enough to make a grown man beg for mercy. It is questionable whether the fiery treatment healed the patient or if the fear of a second treatment drove him to arise the next morning with a determined grin and the announcement, "I am well. I can go to school."

Cough medicine was made from a simple recipe: sugar moistened with kerosene. When a cough persisted this was the undisputed answer to the need. It cured many a hacking cough and saved many sleepless nights for parents and patient, as well as sisters or brothers who had to share the bed or bedroom with the afflicted one. If some student came to school with a bad cough that disturbed the class, the teacher sent a note home with him asking the mother to send coal oil (kerosene) and sugar with him the next day.

Castor oil was a staple on the medicine shelf in every home. The very sight of the bottle was repulsive to all growing children. Like a patient, plotting villain it waited on the shelf, its colorless liquid resting in its bottle ready for the moment its torturous content could be administered to a victim. Little wonder that no child would willingly admit he was constipated. He withheld this information until his discomfort was no longer bearable or until, under ruthless questioning, he was forced to admit his condition. At the moment of his confession his doom was sealed. Walking purposefully to the cabinet, his mother took the castor-oil bottle from the shelf, opened the cabinet drawer where the silverware was stored, took from it a serving spoon — not a teaspoon, a serving spoon — and poured the fatal dose. Then came a brief, but futile, battle of wills. "Swallow this," she said, extending the spoon, which seemed to grow larger as it drew nearer to the mouth. The victim frowned, backed away, and in pleading tones said, "I can't! I can't swallow that!" "Yes, you can and you must. Open wide!" With face screwed up in an agony of tears, the poor patient, with dramatics worthy of a Barrymore, sobbed his denial, pleading to be spared, weeping as if his very life was at stake. The mother was unmoved. "Your performance deserves some kind of award, but you are going to swallow this castor oil," she said, wrapping her tongue around every syllable, "and if you do not swallow it right now, you'll get something to make you wish you had!" Put this way and in that particular tone, he opened and she poured and gagging and sputtering he put it down the little red lane. By next morning he would be feeling peppier than he had in days.

Cuts and other injuries that caused bleeding were treated with a generous daub of turpentine. If it was a deep cut, it was saturated with turpentine and bandaged with clean soft strips of cloth. If turpentine was not available, kerosene was used. Later Cuticura salve was rubbed on it to soften the scabbing. Iodine was often used instead of turpentine, especially if the injury was caused from a nail — particularly a rusty nail. If a sore spot turned into a "risen" (got infected) then a poultice was made from mashed-up madeira leaves and bound to the infected sore by a tightly drawn bandage. Almost every household had a madeira vine growing on a trellis, usually on one end of the porch. It served two purposes — it added beauty and shade and it furnished the necessary leaves for a poultice. And there was always oil of cloves on hand to cure a toothache.

There were many other home remedies which various households held sacred, but those described above were remedies common to all farm households in our area in the '20s.

There were three serious epidemics during those early school days. There was an outbreak of smallpox in

November one year that closed schools all over the county, an epidemic of typhoid fever which kept us closely at home during most of one summer and a very annoying and humiliating siege of itch in the middle of basketball season which brought Ragtown community to its knees. Ours was the only school in the county that suffered this embarrassment. None of the other schools wanted to schedule a basketball game with us nor have anything to do with us in any form or fashion. We were in total disgrace.

Itch is very contagious and because we were constantly together in the classroom and on the playground it was inevitable that most of the student body would be infected. The county health nurse supplied us with a vile-smelling liquid to apply to the infected areas. We were given explicit directions to take it home to our parents because home treatment was essential and strict rules were to be followed if ever we were to be rid of this terrible plague and be able to join the human race again. Finally, our day of absolution came and with it a complete and total purging. All our desks, the floors, the playground equipment, the racks where our coats hung — everything at school — was disinfected with a product that smelled like carbolic acid and worse. Blackboard erasers were burned and new chalk supplied to all the rooms. This was only the beginning — anyone who had been infected with itch must have a certificate from the county health nurse stating that the home had been similarly treated. At home, clothing was washed and treated, beds stripped to the mattress so it could be disinfected, quilts washed, floors scrubbed, furniture cleaned down and sulphur was burned in the rooms. It took all spring to remove the stigma and begin to feel normal again. Cleanliness was stressed in the classroom as it had never been before this experience.

Smallpox broke out before Thanksgiving one year. A wholesale inoculation took place, but too late to prevent it from spreading across the county, reaching epidemic proportions. The men who had served in World War I, or who had been prepared to leave for military service, had been vaccinated, so most men were considered to be immune, but children and women by the hundreds were lined up in the schoolrooms to have their arms scratched and the inoculation administered. Nevertheless, many fell victim. County health officials strode ominously up the front walk of house after house, red cardboard quarantine notices in hand, and nailed them up by the front door. One was nailed on our door because in the second week of the epidemic I was brought home from school in Mr. Robinson's car with a raging fever and by the next morning the telltale pox began to show up all over my body.

It was a harsh, painful, debilitating disease, leaving some victims scarred with pox marks. Dr. Williams and Dr. Sermon were up day and night dispensing ease medicine and carbolated Vaseline. We were instructed to keep the pox saturated with it, and when it itched not to scratch with our fingernails but to rub it with the Vaseline. Because of their vigilant, devoted care most of the county's patients were saved from disfiguring scars and death. Unfortunately, there were some casualties, but none in our community.

When the smallpox epidemic had run its course, the house and its contents were fumigated. After an inspection by the proper authorities, the quarantine sign was removed from the front door. It was like being rid of an unwelcome guest to see that sign go away from the house — it meant life could drop back to normal again.

The summer of the typhoid epidemic was unusually

damp and hot — a humid condition which encouraged mosquitos to breed at an unusual rate. Our water barrel, which sat under the eave of the house to catch rainwater, was drained and turned upside down. When it rained, as it did more frequently that summer, we were not allowed to wade in the puddles and ditches. Although all the water in Garza County was deep well water, all farms had large storage tanks which collected water when the windmills pumped. Since this could create a mosquito problem, we were required to boil all our drinking water.

Children were kept at home and away from crowds. Grown-ups went into town only when necessary. It was a grim summer — tense, with an atmosphere of dread and anxiety. But this, too, passed. Fall arrived and with it the end of the epidemic.

Death came in spite of all the dedicated care and prayers. Friends, loved ones and, sadly, playmates died. It is one of the inevitables of life all children in all ages have had to face and come to terms with.

My first memorable experience with death came one spring before school was out when I was about eight and a playmate, Mozelle, came down with diphtheria. This was a dread sickness that children were susceptible to. It was a diagnosis that no parent could hear without panic, for it was more often fatal than any other childhood disease. To say the word in the presence of a mother was to hear her quickly draw in her breath and cast an anxious look at her child.

Mozelle was a happy, pretty, friendly girl — one of those rare personalities that was fair and kind to everyone and always seemed to be laughing and happy. She was a favorite with both classmates and teachers. She was a special friend to me because her home was just across the field from my grandparents' home, so when I was at their house, she would walk across the field to come and play with me.

It was in the springtime when she became ill. She had been absent from school several days when our classmate, Irene, Mozelle's cousin, told us the ominous and shocking news — she was sick with diphtheria. A shiver of fear ran through our little cluster of friends. Our normal, gay conversation dropped to hushed, hesitant words as a mournful dread settled over us. Day after day we looked at her empty desk, a sadness surrounding it, as we waited for Irene to get to school and give us a report on Mozelle's progress. Then the day came when Irene, too, was absent. When we got home from school that day we were told by our parents the awful truth — Mozelle was dead. I can still remember the dull, throbbing pain of anguish I carried with me for days. A lingering sadness invaded my dreams at night and colored all my waking hours — a harsh, bitter reality.

At school we talked about it for days. A controversy arose over what Mozelle's last words were to her mother. Someone said, "She said 'O, Mama, don't let the hearse get me'." This made Irene mad. "I'm her cousin and I guess I ought to know what she said." She would not tell us what it was since it was nobody's business, she said. All this kind of talk and discussion was great therapy for Mozelle's classmates. It furnished a needed release of our fears, misgivings, sadness and the unreality of her death, for we could talk with each other in a way we could not with our parents or teacher.

Likewise, the student body suffered when one of the

Roland boys died from pneumonia. He was a school favorite, playing basketball and other athletics, one of the older boys and a hero to the younger students. A special hero to me — the handsome, talented older boy that I daydreamed about. So it was a devastating blow when one morning at school I saw the grown-up girls crying and the boys looking grim, their faces white and solemn — we were told that the Roland boy had died. I was sick at heart and asked Miss Hennington if I could go home. When she asked why, I told her I felt sick. She placed her hand on my forehead and found it cool and normal. She asked me if I hurt anywhere and when I said no she finally convinced me I should stay at school. It was a subdued student body all day. No one had the heart to play games. Classroom recitations were a welcome relief to our stricken minds. School let out the next day for the funeral.

Funerals were a ritual of respect for the dead which we were required to attend. The experience was agonizing but as our parents pointed out to us, if we were lying in the casket we would want people to come to our funeral. Logical thinking but poor comfort to a child in grade school.

Word of a death in the neighborhood was quickly passed from household to household, and neighbors hurriedly began to gather at the bereaved home. By nightfall friends and neighbors would have filled the kitchen of the bereaved family with food. The relatives would have been notified and soon would be arriving. Caring hands dressed and "laid out" the corpse in the front room. Several friends or relatives would keep vigil over the body throughout the night. Volunteers would go out early the next morning to dig the grave either in a family plot or in Terrace Cemetery, east of Post.

Back then when a loved one died, friends and relatives wept and the neighbors wept with them. It was a time to grieve and folk were allowed the privilege. When Mr. Easter died as the result of a kick in the chest from one of his mules, friends and neighbors arrived to find his five robust sons pacing the backyard, sobbing loudly and cursing the mule with words most of us had never heard before. (It was also to witness Mrs. Easter clinging doggedly to the shotgun and refusing to allow her determined sons to shoot the mule.) Neighbors mingled their tears and indignation at the criminal mule with those of the boys and when it was all over everybody felt better. After a funeral the bereaved would return home, cry some more and talk about the departed loved one until their systems were relieved. Tears, talking and sobbing have great therapeutic value. Finally, the last tears would be wiped away and the surviving family members could be done with mourning and take up the living of their days.

A funeral was a community affair. The farmers quit the fields and farmwives put aside housework as they all gathered at the white frame church in Ragtown to pay their respects to the dead and to the family of the dead. They stood outside the church until the casket was moved inside. It was either brought to the church on a flatbed wagon pulled by the family's mules and driven by a member of the family, on a farm truck or in a hearse, depending upon the affluence of the family. After the casket and the family were inside the church the people filed in and took their seats. As soon as the singing began the flower girls brought in the sprays and bouquets. They walked down the aisle single file and one by one placed the flowers on the casket or on the floor beside it. A special pew was reserved for them because they would carry the flowers out after the service, walking behind the casket and family. The flower girls were often daughters of the friends of the deceased or young relatives.

While the funeral was going on one or two neighbor women stayed behind and rearranged the furniture in the room where the person died. This was very important. The rationale behind this custom is lost to history; I only know it was one of the functions of the funeral procedure which was unfailingly performed. However, when my grandma died Grandpa would not allow anything to be changed. He stated emphatically that everything was to be left as it was. His request, of course, was honored.

Kids run; kids have always run, they do not need a reason, but back then nobody past the age of sixteen ran unless there was some kind of bad news — a mule had the colic and a neighbor's help was needed to drench him, the cows had broken through the fence into the winter wheat and were eating themselves into a stage of bloat, or Brown's old Jersey bull had escaped from his pasture. If you saw a grown man or woman running down a road it struck fear in your heart. It meant something was seriously wrong — there had been an accident, some family member had been taken suddenly ill, someone had dropped dead or, God forbid, a barn or house was on fire.

It was so on a balmy June day when we saw Mr. Morris, our neighbor to the west, running up the drive into our backyard. Mr. Morris, heaving and panting under the strain of his considerable girth, gasped out, "Fluitt's house is on fire!" "Oh, God!" was Uncle's reply as he headed on the run to the garage to crank up our Model-T Ford. Mr. Morris jumped into the seat beside him as Uncle backed into the road at a dizzying speed and raced toward Fluitt's farm, a few miles west of us, leaving a fog of dust behind.

By the time they arrived close neighbors were already there with buckets, rubber hoses, old quilts, cotton sacks or anything that could be used to beat out a blaze or red-hot embers, hoping to save the house, but if not, smother out or douse any embers that flew onto the barn, outbuildings or haystacks. The direction the wind was blowing was critical for if it blew away from the farmyard other farm buildings were less likely to catch fire. If the wind was blowing toward the farmyard, everything could go up in flames. Fire was the greatest dread a farm family had. We were coached from an early age to be careful and respectful of matches, lamps and stoves.

When a family was burned out the neighbors for miles around dug deep into their household supplies and gave freely and gladly whatever they could spare. Pots, pans, quilts, bedsheets, towels, lye soap, a chair, a mattress. It was not that any family had a surplus of supplies, but they gave what they could do without — if two children could share a bed then the extra one went to the victims. Friends, family and the Good Lord were the only insurance a dry-land farmer had back in those days, for he could not afford any other.

When Fluitt's house was ready to be rebuilt, once again the neighbors were there, this time with saw and hammer in hand ready to begin building. A dozen able-bodied farmers could make short shrift of putting up a house. Soon the victim would move out of the makeshift living quarters in the barn, smokehouse or tent and into a new home complete with all the donations that had been collected to fill it. The woman of the house might recognize a chair or table or lamp from a neighbor's house or a quilt she helped to quilt at some neighbor's house last August. It made her keenly aware of the bond that binds folk together — caring that gives no second thought but opens hearts and hands spontaneously, freely and generously.

The tragedy was no less traumatic if it was a barn that burned. This could mean a loss of valuable feed put away for winter feeding, all the harness for the mules, shelter for the animals as well as storage space. Too often, the haystacks were impossible to save, for most farmers stacked the feed near the lots to be convenient to throw the bundles to the stock. If the wind was in the wrong direction it could also mean the pigsty and hen house would burn. In this case, it was a familiar sight to see a wagonload of bundled feed or maize or a half load of corn pass by on the road to the burned-out farmer. When time came to rebuild the barn, the farmers were there ready to work.

There were also money gifts when disaster struck a farm family. It seldom amounted to more than a hundred or hundred and fifty dollars but that amount of money in the '20s could seem like a fortune to someone who had been wiped out.

It was a sobering experience having a burn-out. For weeks afterwards a kind of sadness clung to the area. Yet, through the tragedy, we were reassured that ours was a generous and helpful community made up of caring friends and neighbors.

It was during these times of experiencing tragedies of death, loss, sickness that we children absorbed the essence of the character of folks that made up our community, the courage and fortitude, the serene acceptance of fate and the poise and good humor with which they dealt with day-to-day living. Great folk they were, these early farm families of the West Texas plains. This greatness was implanted into the roots of that part of Texas, roots that have brought honor to all the seasons in all the years that have passed.

RED LETTER DAYS

Special days and special events were scattered throughout the year. Some were seasonal and some were not. These were happenings outside and in addition to regular and expected holidays which were marked prominently in red letters and numerals on most calendars.

In December the First National Bank at Post handed out new calendars to their customers. They were not decorative like the ones the two drugstores and Greenfield's Hardware Store handed out. Theirs had a beautiful scene or a Norman Rockwell-type picture on it, but the bank's had only its name and slogan printed in prominent letters where a picture might have been. The calendar pages were printed with bold black letters and numerals, except the holidays which were red; New Year's Day, Lincoln's and Washington's birthdays celebrated separately in February, Easter in either March or April, Memorial Day on May thirtieth, July Fourth, Labor Day on the first Monday in September, Armistice Day and Thanksgiving Day in November, Christmas Day in December and Sunday every week. Texas celebrated two holidays that no other state had — Texas Independence Day on the second of March and San Jacinto Day on April twenty-first.

Our bank calendar hung on the pantry wall directly in line with Uncle's place at the kitchen table and just above the striking clock that set on the china cabinet.

None of the community red-letter days appeared on a calendar, but this did not mean they were less important, at least to us. Some followed a routine: wash on Monday, iron on Tuesday, go to town on Saturday. Some were seasonal like hog-killing time. Hog killing was planned after a good hard freeze so the meat would keep until we could get it cured. Pie suppers and box suppers could happen anytime through the year. Some Sunday School class or a school project or the Woman's Home Demonstration Club would need to raise money and the next thing we knew a box supper or an ice cream social was announced. Dinners-on-the-ground at the churches were held in the summer, usually in August. After the corn was harvested in the fall was the time to have the year's supply of cornmeal ground. There were other red-letter events, events we knew would happen but not when, nor in any particular sequence.

The two-story red brick schoolhouse hovered over the collection of houses and buildings that made up Ragtown, the metropolis of my childhood. It was here the important events of my growing-up years transpired; it's where I went to school, to church and to all the special events that made up my social life and the social interchange between the farm families who lived in the community. Pie suppers, box suppers and ice cream socials were held at Ragtown in either the school building or one of the churches. These red-letter socials were announced in the same way that all community announcements were made — word was passed from friend to friend, announced at school during Thursday morning chapel, at the churches on Sunday, and a notice was nailed up on Mr. Parrish's store. By the time the date of the event arrived everyone for miles around had been talking about it for days.

It took some preparation to get ready for one of these events. Pies had to be baked, or the box supper prepared, or a cake baked to go with the freezer of ice cream. The children in the family were admonished at the breakfast table on the morning of the event to polish their shoes. Later on in the day, water was dipped from the rain barrel and put to heat for the ladies and girls to wash their hair; fathers and sons were reluctantly coerced into doing the same. Sunday dresses were brought from the closet and pressed and dad's Sunday clothes brushed and laid out on the bed for his last-minute convenience. Usually, this kind of an occasion called for baths all the way around that would have to be scheduled and commenced early in the afternoon if there were several in the family. Supper had to be prepared and served; the evening chores would have to be done earlier than usual.

Since every female in a family was expected to bring a box to the box supper, preparation for this event took a good deal of time. The box would hold supper for two and could be any container that was suitable for holding the food; however, it must be decorated, that meant "decorated" with a capital D. Since it would be auctioned off, the more beautiful the box, the higher the bidding. Much time, thought and effort went into creating unusual and lavish decorations. Work on the box must be finished long before the appointed day for there were too many other preparations the day of the supper to do justice to it. Crepe paper was the favorite material for covering, but some surprises always turned up. One year Frances Brandon collected the tinfoil from gum wrappers, Hershey candy bars and cigarette packages for weeks, saving it for the time when she would be decorating a box. When it finally made its appearance at the supper it stood out like a bright light in the midst of all the crepe paper. Her current boyfriend had no problem identifying it. For these events it was necessary to have a good auctioneer. Mr. Mason was the favorite choice. He had a good line of patter and not a bit of stage fright. He was the father of the musical Masons who played when we had school programs. They were pressed into service for these occasions and came bringing their banjo, guitar and mandolin, gathering around the school piano and delighting us with their happy music.

The bidding was always brisk between the sparking-age young folk. Everyone knew who was coupled up and that each boy would be bidding to get his favorite girl's box. And all through the bidding the girl would be holding her breath, on pins and needles, for fear someone else would buy her box. If some of the men wanted to create a little fun they would enter the bidding and watch the anxious face of some young man who had a limited amount of money to bid and was desperate to get his girl's box. Once Gomer Custer paid five dollars for Erma Lee Cass' box, did that ever create talk! Five dollars was a lot of money in those days.

Of course, no one was supposed to know whose box they were bidding on, but if a boy wanted a special girl's box she would describe it to him as best she could or she would mark it in some way so it would be easy to identify — a blue ribbon tied around a pink crepe-paper-covered box, or an artificial yellow flower attached to the center. Even then, sometimes the boy misunderstood her code and ended up with the wrong box.

When a sale was final, the purchaser went up to the auctioneer, paid his bid and collected his box. When they all were sold the one who prepared the box found her partner and the box was opened to reveal all the good stuff inside. It would be filled with fried chicken, or slices of roast beef, or ham sandwiches, potato salad, deviled eggs, spiced pickled peaches, cake, homemade candy and cheese and crackers. Anyone who bought a box knew he would have a sumptuous supper regardless of who he ate with, so a good time was had by all.

A pie supper was less festive but looked forward to just as eagerly. Parents were more involved in it than the young folk though they would be present in large numbers. It was just what the name implies, pie for supper. The women baked their favorite pies to be auctioned off. There would be some mouth-watering beauties lined up on the table to go under the auctioneer's gavel. Cream pies, chocolate, lemon, and coconut topped with high peaked meringue delicately browned so that little golden beads of sugar, like morning dew, clung to its hills and valleys. There would be chess pies, a delicious mixture of eggs, creamy milk, sugar and a touch of nutmeg for flavor.

And pecan pie with the chunky nuts lying tantalizingly in a rich, brown filling made from Karo, sugar and eggs. Raisin, apple, peach and berry would complete the selection with their flaky crusts browned to a turn and decorated with whimsical designs punched in with a fork.

Whoever bought a pie could take it home or eat it on the spot. Mostly, the boys ate theirs right then and there; sometimes two or three pooled their money to buy one and, more often than not, ended up in a row over the proper division of the spoils.

It was the same with the ice cream social. This was the Woman's Home Demonstration Club specialty. Every member of the club brought a freezer of ice cream and a cake to go along with it. The ice cream was sold by the bowl and the cake was sold by the slice. This put the sale items within reach of everyone's pocketbook. A person could buy as many bowls of ice cream or pieces of cake as he or she could afford.

Along with these looked-forward-to events, there were the dinner-on-the-ground Sundays. This was a summer function and both the churches at Ragtown held at least one or more every summer. A dinner-on-the-ground was a community and intercommunity affair. People came from the Graham Chapel or Pleasant Valley communities to attend church that Sunday and stayed for the feast and fun. Folk from our community would show up at the Grassland community church when they held a dinner. It was possible to attend several during the summer months. Some Sundays after dinner was over everyone went back inside the church and sang until folk had to go home to do the evening chores. The kids who did not want to sing or were not required by their parents to go inside, could stay outside and organize games, always with a few adults sitting in the shade of the church, talking and keeping an eye out for any misbehavior that might develop.

On these special Sundays, church was held in the usual manner with a capacity crowd in attendance, their minds half on the worship service and half on the treat to follow. After the final "Amen," everyone spilled out of the church to the backyard where long boards had been placed across sawhorses to make as many tables as necessary. It was like the July Fourth celebration; every family brought big boxes and baskets of food. This time, however, it would be spread on a common table. The meat dishes were all arranged at one end of the table, the salads and vegetables next, then the bread, and on the far end were the numerous tempting desserts. The boards groaned and creaked under the heavy load. The lines moved slowly, discriminately down the length of the food and at the end, plates were piled high with all kinds of good stuff. Kids loved it for there was no one to notice, in all the commotion, that they were eating dessert first. It was a fun time, lots of fellowship and laughter and reunions with seldom-seen friends from neighboring communities. Kids chased each other and scuffled good naturedly while a few neighborhood dogs showed up to take advantage of discarded plates, dropped chicken bones and tidbits of pie and cake. A great institution, dinner-on-the-ground. Whoever thought it up must surely have a special place in Heaven.

Whenever a farm family installed a telephone it was a red letter day. Telephones appeared fairly rapidly once the trend was started. All of us could remember when there were none in the community, so when a new one was installed the news passed from household to household that Morrises or Meadors or some other neighbor got a phone put in. It was exciting news. Those who already had phones rang them up so they could try out their new acquisition. A main telephone line ran by our house. Three wires ran through blue glass insulators attached to the crossbar at the top of the poles. When the atmosphere was just right the wind blew through the wires and set up a humming that could be heard as far away as the barn lot. If you stood under the wire or walked too close the noise could be deafening.

When the line was first installed we and the Hendersons had the only telephones in our neighborhood, but before many months had gone by there were six or seven parties on our line. The convenience and luxury was something to boast about — nothing short of a miracle that we could so quickly and easily communicate over long distances. Why, a person could talk to somebody as far away as Dallas and, truth was, even as far away as New York City.

The phone itself was a large box-type instrument made of oak wood which had been stained and varnished. It had a crank on the right side, a hook holding the receiver on the left side, and at the front was a large horn extending forward like an overgrown nose. Above the horn were two large silver-colored bells looking for the world like two huge eyes. This remarkable instrument was attached to a wall, usually in the front room, at a height convenient for an adult to stand and talk with ease. When you wanted to make a call to someone you held down the hook and turned the crank one long turn for Central. Central was the operator who sat at the switchboard in the central office at Post. Placing the receiver to your ear and positioning your mouth to speak into the horn, you waited for Central to answer. "Number, please?" she asked; then you gave her the number you wanted to call. She plugged you in with the proper party and rang that number.

As soon as you rang Central it alerted everyone on the line and most folk took their receivers down, prepared to listen in on the conversation. It's easy to understand why kids back then did not hang on the phone passing secrets and philosophy back and forth to each other. With that kind of chaperonage we took care of our business as promptly as possible and hung up.

Old-fashioned party lines, however, had their advantages. When there was an emergency it was quick work to get the word out. If the phone rang late at night (an alarming thing), one of my parents, as did others on the line, got out of bed to listen in, no matter whose ring, to learn what the trouble was. No one would make a phone call after bedtime unless it was an emergency. Our worst dread was getting a long-distance call. This meant someone was seriously ill or a relative was at "death's door" or already dead. When a neighbor was sick Auntie often lifted the receiver to listen to the progress report. If it wasn't a good report she might "butt in." "Do you need me to come and sit up?" or "Do you need Mr. Mangum to go get medicine for you?" or whatever offer was appropriate.

One of Auntie's friends phoned one day and asked her to read off her applesauce cake recipe. Before she started reading the list of ingredients one of the women on the line said, "Oh, do wait a minute! Let me get my pencil and paper so I can write it down, too." In the middle of reading the ingredients, another voice "butted in": "It sure improves the cake to put in a pinch of soda." When Auntie hung up she was mad as a hornet. "She's got her nerve! Old Buttinsky! My applesauce cake does not need improving!"

It was not uncommon, if a conversation lingered on,

for someone on the line to "butt in" and say, "Would you mind getting off the line? I need to use the phone." The parties, being polite, hung up. However, as soon as "Butt In" rang Central, down came the receivers to find out what this important call was all about.

It was possible to ring someone on your line without going through Central. Our number was a long and two shorts. So if Mrs. Brown wanted to call Auntie all she had to do was hold down the hook and turn one long crank and two short cranks and our telephone would ring. Almost as good as Touch-tone dialing. Everyone on the line knew all the "rings" so it was not blind guessing when a telephone rang, we all knew who was receiving a call.

We also knew more about our neighbor's business than we would have otherwise known. We knew that Mrs. Mosley was expecting to receive a handsome settlement from an insurance company as a result of an injury to her shoulder in a car accident on her way home from Abilene. We knew when the Easleys' decided to sell their farm. Though we were not listening in, one of Uncle's friends was, so as soon as he could get the phone he called to tell him. Uncle was down there within the hour making his offer because it adjoined our farm and he had long hoped for just this opportunity. We knew that one of the neighborhood widow women was carrying on with one of the town men, for she got calls that were heavily coded and soon after she hung up we would see her car pull out of her long drive and head off toward Post. We knew when the Johnsons' sharp-tongued aunt was coming from Waxahachie to visit. It was a long-distance call so she made it short and to the point, "I'll be there Monday. Be sure to meet the train. Don't be late," she admonished them sharply and with a benedictory click hung up the telephone. Though we could not hear their comments, we knew there would be no joy in the Johnson household over that announcement.

The advent of the telephone in our rural area brought changes in our lives, subtle changes, which were our first step out into the big world.

One of the things we did not buy at Mr. Childress' store was cornmeal. We took our own corn to Mr. Thomas to be ground into coarse, whole-grained meal which Auntie would bake into corn bread. She cooked it in a black iron skillet and brought it straight from the oven to the table. The thick, hot slices, opened to take a generous slab of butter, were delicious served with fresh vegetables or red beans.

Uncle and I would load the back of the wagon with shucked ears of corn, hitch up Dinah and Jack, climb over the front wheels onto the wagon seat and head out for the Thomas farm about a mile and a half away. Looking past the telephone lines and to the southwest, we could see "Hound Dog" Thomas' place crouching in the distance. He got the name "Hound Dog" because he was the only man in the community who owned hound dogs. There were always several of them and when they set to baying on a summer night the noise disturbed every household for miles around. The hounds would hear us pull into the yard and come scrambling from under the back porch, tumbling over each other as they raced toward the wagon, baying with every breath. All this commotion brought Mr. Thomas out of the house, yelling at the hounds to shut up. After this noisy fanfare, it seemed anticlimactic to announce we had come only to have our corn ground. As we left, the hounds had another go at it and gave us a rousing send-off.

Most families set aside a week for hog killing. This was after the weather had decidedly turned to winter. Since we had no artificial refrigeration we depended upon nature's refrigeration, cold weather, to keep the meat from spoiling until it could be processed. Most farm families required that two hogs be slaughtered in order to provide sufficient meat for the farm table throughout the year, but Uncle and Grandpa killed only one and divided it between our two households.

In preparation for the butchering, Auntie sewed long, slim muslin sacks for stuffing the sausage and Grandpa got the smokehouse cleaned and ready. The smokehouse was a small square frame building built especially for storing and curing meat; large hooks were attached to the rafters and the meat and sausages were hung from these hooks. The curing mixtures for the hams, shoulders and bacon must be mixed, along with the sausage seasoning — making sure to put in the right amount of sage and not too much red pepper. Uncle sharpened the knives and checked out the meat grinder and made sure the scalding vat was in place on the north side of the windmill. He must make sure the pulley was attached securely to one of the cross-bars near the top of the mill. This arrangement was for hanging the hog so he could be disemboweled, so it must be strong enough to support considerable weight. This was the last indignity the poor animal suffered after being stabbed to death, scalded in boiling water and the hair shaved from his body. Butchering a hog is not a pleasant subject.

The first day of hog killing started before sunup and lasted until time to do evening chores; by then we would be ready for the actual processing which would take place over the next several days. The meat for the sausage had to be ground, mixed with the seasoning, stuffed into the sacks and tied tightly at the top. The hams and shoulders had to be trimmed and the curing mixture rubbed into them by hand. The bacon had to have its own special treatment just right, without too much salt. Numerous steps were required to get the full benefit from a hog, making sure to preserve every part possible. Certain portions were ground and made into souse and then shaped into a loaf. The natural gelatin in this part of the meat caused it to congeal so that it could be cut into thin slices and served with a sprinkling of vinegar. Very good with vegetables. The sweetbreads were prepared on the spot and served with the first meal after the processing was finished. The spareribs and loin were the choice parts and were kept in the window cooler where they would not spoil before they could be eaten. When the backbone was cooked, the last part with dumplings maybe, the marrow that came from the bones was a real tasty delicacy. The excess fat, cut away from the many parts throughout the entire preparation, was divided so the choice white fat could be rendered into lard which would be used to make pie crust, biscuits and other bread. The less desirable portions of the fat were thrown into the big black wash pot, covered and left there to be made into lye soap at a later date. With a heavy object placed on the lid so the dogs and cats could not get to it, it could be left indefinitely until it was convenient for the housewife to make it into soap. I stayed well out of the way on hog-killing day; the violence of it made me feel sick. I appeared on the scene about the time Auntie and Aunt Mattie were ready to grind the sausage, the only part I cared to participate in or was allowed to help with. The grinder was fastened to the cabinet top with a large turn key. It was fun to turn the handle and watch the strands of ground pork come out at the front.

Whatever curing they did kept the meat edible so that we had delicious bacon, sausage and ham well into the spring of the year. When we got down to the last of the hams and bacon, green splotches were to be seen here and there on them but this did not alarm Auntie and Aunt Mattie. They took a sharp knife and cut these parts out, going deep to be sure and get all the spoiled part and the meat was then cooked and eaten in the usual way. No one ever got sick from eating it.

After the hog meat was satisfactorily stored and all the implements used in the process put away, the housewife could turn her attention to soap making. On soap-making day one of the young family members was sent to the pasture to gather dried cow chips, carrying a tow sack for hauling them back to the house. These were piled around the black iron pot, a little kerosene was poured on them and soon there was a good roaring hot fire. Several cans of lye were dumped into the fat scraps and as soon as it began to get hot the housewife, or some appointed older child, would stand over the pot with a cut-off broom handle and begin stirring — and stir and stir and stir. The proportions of lye to fat and the diligent stirring was what turned out firm, pale golden-yellow soap.

When the soap was finished, it was left in the pot and allowed to set until it was firm all the way through; then it was cut into pieces that could be easily handled. It was used for washing dishes, clothing, linens and, at times, for washing one's hair. My Aunt Rosa, who had exceptionally nice skin, washed her face with it every night before going to bed. She did this from the time I can remember to age ninety-two, when she died. It easily cut farm dirt and grease out of overalls and soiled play clothes, yet, it was not too harsh for sheets and pillowcases, print dresses and Sunday shirts. Even after P&G soap bars and Ivory Flakes made their entrance into our lives, lye soap was still a standard washday product.

Out on the farm in the '20s in West Texas the only washing machine we knew about was a bench with two big galvanized tubs sitting on it. Ours sat under the mulberry tree, our special place to do the washing. Mrs. Meador kept her wash bench on the back porch and the two tubs hung on the wall above it along with the metal headgear that had been part of Mr. Meador's military uniform when he was a soldier in World War I. Some women had a wash house. Aunt Clara had one in her backyard. A little shed where her wash bench, tubs, rub board and a special stove for heating water were kept. She had an oval-shaped copper boiler to boil her clothes in rather than the black iron pot, sitting on stubby little legs in the backyard, that most women used.

If at all humanly possible, washing was done on Monday morning. About the only thing that would interfere with this routine was a sandstorm or the rare occasions when it rained. Once again a young family member was sent on an errand to the cow pasture, his tow sack thrown over his shoulder, to pick up dried chips. While he was on his safari, the black pot would be filled with water and some lye soap shavings added. Cow chips make a very hot fire and this is what was needed to bring the water up to a boil. A full milk bucket of this hot water was dipped out into one of the tubs and enough cold water added to make it just right for washing the clothes. The tub sitting next to it was filled with cold water for rinsing and to it was added some bluing. The bluing was for giving the final assurance that the white clothes would be snowy white when they were hung on the line to dry.

Preparations complete, the rub board was positioned in the tub of warm water and the actual washing began. White clothes were washed first — the Sunday shirts, white underwear, any white garments, pillowcases and sheets. Each piece was pushed down into the water then lifted up dripping wet onto the wash board, rubbed with a bar of the lye soap, scrubbed up and down the board until it was judged to be clean. Then it was wrung out and dropped into the pot of boiling water where it was allowed to "simmer until done." While the whites were boiling, the print dresses, blouses and other underwear were washed on the rub board, rinsed and, if necessary, starched.

The starch had been made in the kitchen and brought to the wash bench in the dishpan. It was made by mixing just the right amount of starch and water and cooking it on the stove until thick. After it was removed from the burner enough water would be added to thin it to the right consistency for starching school dresses, shirts, aprons, pillowcases and housedresses. These articles had been washed, rinsed, starched and hung on the clothesline by the time the white clothes had finished boiling. The white clothes were then fished out of the water and brought back to the washtub for inspection and to have the hot water wrung from them before they were placed into the rinsing tub. After the white clothes were removed from the pot the overalls and work shirts were put into the boiling water for their turn.

It was not an easy job to wash clothes. Garments and bed clothing that were full of water were heavy. Not only did each piece have to be lifted, but it must be pushed and pulled with force, "elbow grease," as we called it, up and down on the rub board, then the water squeezed out before it could be dropped into the rinse water. Here each piece was plunged up and in the water until it had all the soap rinsed from it; then it had to be wrung out and maybe put through the starch water, in which case it had to be wrung a third time. As soon as a basketful was ready it would be carried to the lines and each piece attached to the line with clothespins. After that final step it was up to the wind and sun to dry everything. In spite of all the hard work, however, there was a sense of pride and pleasure at seeing a line full of clean linens. When they were dry and taken off the line there was the sweet smell of them, for which there are no words for describing the heavenly, fresh aroma that clings to clothes that have dried outside in the sunshine and fresh air. It is the reward for all the hard work.

Of course, we all knew that on Tuesday we ironed our clothes. How those women's eyes would have popped could they have plugged an iron into an outlet and in a few seconds have it be hot at a predetermined temperature. And they would have been totally amazed had it shot out steam and had there been an aerosol can to spray the starch.

Early that morning, or the night before, all the clothing and linens to be ironed were sprinkled with water (every household had its sprinkle bottle) and rolled up tightly in a large cloth so they would absorb the dampness all the way through. Proper sprinkling was necessary if the wrinkles were to be taken out when the piece was ironed. The irons, most households had three, were set across one of the burners on the kerosene stove. When one was thought to be hot enough to iron with, the handle was attached, or the lifting pad used if the handle was not detachable, to lift the iron off the burner. To test whether the iron was hot enough, a finger was touched to the tongue and quickly applied to the bottom of the iron. If it was hot enough to sizzle spit then you were ready to begin ironing. The ironing board was placed between two chairs, resting on the topmost part, or on the edge of the kitchen table and a chair top. It did not take long for an iron to cool down, so during the time it took to finish an ironing there were many a trip made between stove and board to exchange a cool iron for a hot one.

Ironing was not an easy task either. It meant standing over the board for long tedious hours, and in the summer it was a very hot job. But women took pride in starched and beautifully ironed dresses, in a crisply ironed table runner and in feeling their husband's shirt front looked glossier and smoother than any other in church on Sunday morning. Some women even went so far as to iron the sheets and cup towels. When the ironing board was put away on Tuesday evening, it was with a proud, fine feeling of accomplishment that the weekly chore of washing and ironing was over and done with and hand and mind could be turned to other activities.

Another regularly scheduled event was the Saturday bath. This took some doing. First one of the galvanized washtubs was brought inside and set on the kitchen floor if it was wintertime or into the back bedroom if it was summer. The kettle and two or three pots were filled with water and put on the kitchen cookstove to get hot. A clean towel, washcloth and a bar of soap, Castile at our house, were put beside the tub on a chair. When the water was hot the operation began. The one to bathe first got the clean water. Since there were only three of us and I was usually the first to bathe, I did not know, except through what I was told by my friends from big families, what it was like to get into a tub that several others had already used. There were bitter complaints that certain members of the family had more first turns than others and that some bathers abused the privilege as well as the water in the tub. It was highly entertaining to be told about; nevertheless, I was secretly glad I did not have to deal with the problem. And, of course, the larger one was, the harder it was to get the body folded up enough to fit into a number three washtub. It was certainly not a very luxurious way to bathe but it was the only way we farm kids knew. However crude the facilities, it was refreshing to get the water all over one's body and dry off all over with a nice soft towel.

Once a week was as often as we bathed in the tub. The other days we "washed up as far as possible and down as far as possible," using the wash pan and washrag at the kitchen sink, before we went to bed at night when we were in school or when we were "going somewhere" other times.

Hand in glove with bathing was hair washing. That was the purpose of the rain barrel. Most rain barrels were made of wood staves held together with circular bands of iron, and one sat under an eave of every farmhouse (ours sat by the back door) to catch the water that ran off the roof when it rained. It was hoped it would rain enough throughout the year to keep plenty in the barrel, not only for washing hair but for washing delicate things; a white linen detachable collar, things with lots of lace on them, the silk stockings belonging to the lady of the house. Little kids liked to hang on the rim and pull themselves up to see their reflection in the water, holler into it to hear the dull echo of their voice, or see if water was the only thing inside the barrel. We were forbidden to do this, of course, for we might fall in and drown.

Water that was pumped from the well was delicious to drink and good for most household uses but it was hard, and when used to shampoo it left the hair tangled and dull, whereas the rainwater left it soft and manageable and with a glossy sheen. So hair-washing day was another event that entailed preparation. First, the kettle was filled with rainwater and put on the stove to get hot. A bucketful was set on the sink for cooling down the water to a comfortable temperature. Soap and towel were placed within easy reach. The pan that sat in the sink for washing hands, feet and face was filled when the water was ready. The head leaned low over the pan and the eyes squinched up so no soap would get into them. Then the water was sloshed by the handful over and into the hair until it was wet, the soap rubbed on it until a good lather was worked up. The final result of scrubbing and rinsing and towel drying was a good clean head of hair. If it was summertime we went outside to let it dry in the sun; if it was winter we stayed by the heating stove until it was dry. This head-washing ritual was performed in the same manner for boys, girls and parents. My boy cousins complained bitterly over the ordeal but to no avail; mothers soaped and scrubbed their scalps as vigorously as they did the girls'.

Many facets of that era, the '20s, would disappear in the '30s. It would fill volumes, these threads of the past that wound their way throughout my young years and out of my life.

1929

Why did they have to go? I asked Auntie, as my cousins were lost to view down the county road, waving from the car windows until gone from sight. I was not near ready for their visit to be over and I already missed them. Back inside the house, it seemed large and empty and I was lonesome.

"I know you will be lonesome for awhile, but they had to go home, you know," she said, then added, "all good things must come to an end." When I was much older I understood the literal interpretation of this old adage: Change is the only constant in life.

A dramatic change in our way of life

came with the 1929 stock-market crash. The echo from the crash resounded through the land like the tolling of a death knell. Economists, brokers and congressmen wrung their hands in despair, proposed their theory and wrote and spoke reams of words on why it happened. These theories and words came nowhere near the truth — they were all wrong. We kids who were growing up in West Texas that year knew what brought the crash. There was no doubt in our minds. It was the wind.

It started as a whirlwind one cold, bleak spring day and did not stop until the vast, broad, unending plains became a dust bowl. The great backbone of the country, the plains — where cotton, wheat and cattle flourished and prospered and fed the nation — fell victim to an undefeatable adversary. The wind won its battle. Smoldering in anger and resentment for having to relinquish its waving prairie grass, its buffalo, its delicately leafed mesquite trees, and its uncluttered landscape, it felled its enemy — the farmer. With the farmer stopped dead in his tracks there was no one left to supply the needs of the land. No wonder the world crashed down upon us!

It was a grim time, a *Grapes of Wrath* time. Farmers drove their sand-pocked Model-Ts to town, standing in the Red Cross line or the government assistance line to pick up food rations for their families and farm animals. It was a demeaning thing for proud people to have to do, but it was a choice they had to make — sacrifice pride and eat or go hungry. It was a time of deep suffering of the soul and body for those sturdy West Texas farmers.

"Who has seen the wind?" the poet Christina Rossetti asks in one of her poems. To this day no one has. Nor caught it. Nor tamed it. Nor analyzed it in a laboratory. It drives ships at sea, turns windmills, cools us on hot summer days; it moans around the corners of buildings, snatches books and scarves from girls and boys, sends tumbleweeds rolling against picket fences, stirs up gigantic waves in the midst of the ocean, rips roofs off buildings and roars through the countryside flattening entire towns and leaving death and destruction in its wake. It is a mighty force to deal with.

It brought an end to those golden, storybook days of the '20s, as we knew them on those flat plains of West Texas, an end to a way of life, gone out of existence, never to be experienced again. It was a year to turn around and face the wind — walk straight into it. Time to turn around and let the wind blow.

Helen Mangum Fields moved to the farm of her aunt and uncle in 1919 when she was two years old. Home became a West Texas dry-land farm in Garza County, eight miles west of Post. This is where she spent all of her growing-up years.

Mrs. Fields holds a B.A. from West Texas State College in Canyon, now part of the Texas A&M University system. She and her husband M. William Fields, have four children, nine grandchildren and one great grandchild.

Walking Backward in the Wind is her first book. She is currently working on a novel.